EASTERN NATIONAL

MEMORIES OF A BUS COMPANY

EDITED AND COMPILED BY ANDY GIPSON

This book is dedicated to all
bus workers who have
sacrificed their lives during
the Covid-19 pandemic in 2020.

First published by the Eastern and Southern Branch of The Omnibus Society, a registered charity No. 1048887 in 2020.

The Eastern and Southern Branch was formed in 1988. principally for those members of the society resident in and/or interested in road passenger transport in Bedfordshire, Buckinghamshire, Cambridgeshire, Essex, Hertfordshire, Norfolk, Suffolk, Berkshire, Hampshire, Kent, Oxfordshire, Surrey, Sussex, Isle of Wight and the southern part of Lincolnshire. It also serves Greater London to supplement the facilities provided by the Society meetings in London and those of the London Historical Research Group. Two Bulletins, one each for the Eastern and Southern areas are produced and are regularised so that members receive a bulletin each month. The Bulletins contain news of changes to bus services in their respective areas and details of Society visits, tours and meetings. The branch arranges visits to bus operators with study tours by local service buses. There are two sub-groups which the branch oversees namely Herts and Beds Group and the Essex and South Suffolk Group who both hold meetings on a regular basis.

Find out more and if you wish to join the Omnibus Society, please contact it at

100 Sandwell Street, Walsall WS1 3EB. info@omnibus-society.org

Design and layout:- Carnegie Book Production, Carnegie House, Chatsworth Road, Lancaster, LA1 4SL. carnegiepublishing.co.uk

ISBN: 978 1 90909 127 6

The front and back covers show a map of all Eastern National services in 1945. The front is the Eastern Area and the back is the Midland Area, however there are no services linking the two areas. In June, 1950 this was remedied when Service 164 commenced operations between Bishop's Stortford and Royston, however this was withdrawn by 6th May, 1953, becoming Service 188 operated by the United Counties Omnibus Company Ltd. between Buntingford and Royston. There was a brief link in the 1930's, between May 1938 and December 1939 when Service 40 operated into Royston on Wednesdays only following the takeover of H. Wilson's Clavering and District Motor Services.

Contents

Foreword

Growing up in the North East, and with family holidays in Birmingham or Aldershot, Eastern National meant little to me during childhood. Collecting British Bus Fleets No 4 taught me of strange Bristol MW registration numbers such as 1 BXB or 1865 F but other than that, nothing.

It wasn't until a first job with Eastern Counties in Peterborough and an opportunity to, successfully, take my PSV test in former ENOC FLF 97 TVX that I started to take an interest, and about time too given a Bristol/ECW passion. The new Highwayman network appeared in Peterborough too with a livery to turn heads so a wander to Essex was on the cards.

Looking back now Southend PD3s appear to have, disgracefully, hogged the camera lens but some digging through boxes of slides helped me find MWs in Clacton and Braintree, FLFs in Wood Green and dual purpose VRs in London Victoria. What a fleet.

Fast forward to 1997 and there I was with Arriva the Shires. We had recently gained responsibility for the former Southend Corporation operation who, would you credit it, competed with an Eastern National successor. So now some professional dealings with ENOC, all of which were quite fascinating.

Fast forward yet again to late 2013. Now I'm MD of First in the Midlands. Our legal address is, yes, in Chelmsford. It was, and is, a pleasure to chat with long serving colleagues about all matters Eastern National. Many of those reminiscences have fortunately been included as you read on.

It gives me the greatest of unexpected pleasure now, as Chairman of the Omnibus Society, to offer a few words of congratulation to all those involved in the preparation of this volume. Our UK Bus Managing Director, Giles Fearnley, shares with me pride in the heritage and traditions of successful bus operation that ENOC inherited ninety years ago and now First takes forward into the future. We're both very grateful for the hard work, passion and dedication shown in the compilation of what will be a delightful read.

Nigel Eggleton

Chairman, The Omnibus Society.

Giles Fearnley

Managing Director, First Bus, FirstGroup plc

Foreword

I live in Luton so I am grateful that I have this opportunity to write this foreword about the memory of Eastern National in the "Midland" National area. The starting point was the proposed division of the operating areas of the National Omnibus and Transport Company Ltd. (NOTC), which before 1930 stretched from Cornwall to Essex each with a shareholding by one of the four mainline railway companies.

It soon proved unable to proceed with "Midland" National serving NOTC's operations based on Bedford and Luton as both the LMSR and LNER railways had main lines passing through the area. In the Eastern National area centred on Chelmsford, Essex, it was mainly served by LNER, but the LMSR had the London, Tilbury and Southend line. The solution was a larger Eastern National Omnibus Company Ltd. (ENOC) covering both areas, with equal LMSR and LNER shareholdings, which took over operations in 1930.

From 1933, by now firmly under Tilling control, ENOC and Western/Southern National became largely separate entities, with headquarters at Chelmsford and Exeter respectively. ENOC now registered all of its new vehicles with Essex C.C., having previously registered the "Midland" National vehicles with Bedfordshire C.C. in line with established NOTC practice. For the next 19 years the ENOC "Midland" and "Eastern" areas operated side by side with their own service numbering series, as inherited from NOTC with separate timetable books.

The only local bus route which linked the two areas together was what would become Service 164 between Bishop's Stortford and Royston, which between 1950 and 1953 was operated from the Bishop's Stortford "Eastern" area depot. There were summer coastal express services which would regularly bring "Midland" area vehicles to Clacton-on-Sea and Southend-on-Sea etc. ; it is said that Clacton depot vehicles incorporated Bedford and Luton settings on their destination blinds, just in case they were called upon to provide return duplication at busy times.

The big change came on 1st May, 1952 when a reorganisation of the British Transport Commission bus company areas meant the entire "Midland" area of ENOC was transferred to the Northampton based United Counties Omnibus Company Ltd (UCOC); ENOC had shared a long common boundary with UCOC stretching from Thrapston in the east to Aylesbury in the west. The UCOC vehicle fleet doubled overnight, however there was little evident change in the eyes of this six year old who was already taking an interest in buses and trains. The buses remained in Tilling green livery, with just UCOC fleet number plates, fleetnames etc. Service numbers initially remained the same. Most people in Luton, as with other "border" towns, relied on the handy pocket-sized road/rail timetables regularly published by Index Publishers for London Transport and distributed through local newsagents. The ex ENOC vehicles with their Essex registrations remained a familiar if gradually declining sight in the UCOC area for many years. The very last in service were Bristol KSW5G, TNO 674 and TNO 677 (UCOC 881/2, ex ENOC 4149/52) which brought the curtain down at Bedford in August 1970.

Today there are very few personal memories of the ENOC "Midland" area available, however it is fitting that this commemorative book to mark the 90th anniversary of the creation of ENOC can now be read. My congratulations must be extended to Andy Gipson, Branch Secretary of the Eastern and Southern Branch of the Omnibus Society, who as editor, has brought together all of the various 'memory' contributions. I trust all will find it of interest.

Roger Barton

Omnibus Society-Branch Chairman, Eastern and Southern Branch.

Luton. 2020.

Introduction

Unprecedented. This is a word that has become synonymous during 2020 whilst the Covid-19 pandemic affects the United Kingdom. It might have been used to some extent during 1929 and 1930 when negotiations between the National Omnibus &Transport Company Limited (NOTC) and the "big four" railway companies were undertaken to form a new bus company called the Eastern National Omnibus Company Ltd. The two railway companies being directly affected were the London and North Eastern and the London Midland and Scottish and it all started on 11th April, 1930 following the registration of the Company on 28th February, 1929. NOTC provided the management services from its headquarters at 206 Brompton Road, London SW3 for a short time before moving to the headquarters of Thomas Tilling Ltd. at 20 Victoria Street, London SW1 who took a controlling interest of ENOC in 1931. From 1934, Eastern National established its own Head Office at New Writtle Street, Chelmsford. If the company—often abbreviated to ENOC and used throughout this book—had survived until 2020, it would have celebrated ninety years of public transport service to the people of Essex and in earlier years until 1952 to the people of Bedfordshire and to the old county of Huntingdonshire and areas slightly beyond. Perhaps this achievement alone would have been unprecedented when considering all of the changes which have taken place since the de-regulation of the United Kingdom bus industry in 1986 and the operation of bus services generally.

You will not find a definitive history about ENOC vehicles, services and routes in this book, but a miscellany of stories from people who worked and had an interest in ENOC. You might find some "bus" jargon creeping into the text, jumpers, lurkers, rabbits, scratchers, swingers and OMO (not the washing powder and not now politically correct) for which I apologise; however these are uncensored and interesting accounts of the voices of people who were involved and had an interest with ENOC.

The book is divided into four memory sections with appropriate illustrations:-

A Brief History, Off the buses at "Head Office and Depots", On the buses with "Operating Staff" and with a General Assortment to finish. There is no real need to read the book from cover to cover because in each section you will find out about different pictures of life with a bus company that you might not have been aware of until now. Just indulge yourself in the memories that interest you most of times past.

ENOC Head Office in 1950 opened in 1934 at New Writtle Street, Chelmsford. The building is extant and is known as Stapleford House, occupied by organisations connected with the National Health Service.

A short history of Eastern National

The wheels on the bus go round and round

The history of Eastern National is one of circles

Its origins go back to 1909 when Thomas Clarkson introduced his Chelmsford built steam buses in London as the National Steam Car Co Ltd., becoming the National Omnibus and Transport Co Ltd (NTOC) in 1920, a year after it had agreed with London General to leave London, in exchange for acquiring Bedford!

Eastern National Omnibus Company Limited (ENOC) was registered on 28 February 1929, to take over the Essex and Bedfordshire operations, as a subsidiary of NOTC, the London Midland and Scottish Railway (LMS) and the London & North Eastern Railway (LNER) each acquiring a 25% holding in the new ENOC which commenced operations in 1930.

After nationalisation late in 1948, the British Transport Commission (BTC) reorganised many of its operations. ENOC lost its Grays area operations to London Transport and its Bedfordshire area operations to United Counties in 1952. At the same time ENOC took control of Westcliff-on-Sea Motor Services Ltd, operating in South East Essex, and Brentwood and into North East London. Coordination with the two municipalities in Essex, Southend-on-Sea and Colchester followed in 1954 and 1982 respectively. This was the situation when I joined ENOC in 1984.

In 1985, London Transport services were offered for tender to non LT operators. ENOC returned to London some 66 years after the National Steam Car Co Ltd withdrew, winning contracts for services 193 (operated from Brentwood) and W9 from a new outstation in Enfield. The following year, larger tranches of London contracts were awarded, with new depots at Walthamstow and Ponders End.

The first registered office of ENOC, the former offices of NOTC at 206 Brompton Road Underground Station (Piccadilly Line), London S.W. 3. The entrance to the offices on the first floor of this "L" shaped building was by the central door between the two pillars. This photograph was taken on 3rd June, 1937, following the closure of the station on 30th July, 1934 and after ENOC had left the premises in 1932. Today only the facade of the side elevation situated in Cottage Place (opposite the Brompton Oratory) off the Brompton Road is extant. Note the 'Light & Spacious Rooms' to let sign, rather than office accommodation being available.

A possible Company montage of buses in 1931. Leading from the front No.3088, EV 1224, Leyland TS1 followed by No.2506, VW 2990 Leyland Lion PLSC3 and then probably No.3017, VX 4673 Leyland TS1 and No. 3068, EV 1947 Thorneycroft Daring XC.

An early scene of ENOC buses at Great Bardfield in 1931. No. 3152, TM 9184, a Leyland TD 1 is at the front on what appears to be a private hire outing for the village.

The Transport Act 1985 had two main aims, to promote competition by deregulating services and to privatise the nationalised groups, National Bus Company (NBC) and Scottish Bus Group (SBG). The subsidiaries were to be privatised company by company. ENOC was thus set to return to the private sector. Coordination Agreements such as those at Southend and Colchester were terminated abruptly on deregulation day, 26th October 1986 as such agreements were deemed uncompetitive.

It was, however, not ENOC that was privatised, when its operations passed on to ENOCs senior and middle management in a Management Buy Out (MBO) on 23rd December 1986, just three months after deregulation. Because ENOC was negotiating to sell Southend Victoria Bus Station to Sainsbury's, and to avoid prohibitive delay and legal costs, NBC incorporated a new company in November 1986 to acquire all of ENOC's business and assets with the exception the Southend Victoria site. That company was named Westcliff-on-Sea Motor Services Ltd (Westcliff), a familiar name but not the same company as the one acquired by ENOC in 1952. So 'Eastern National' (ENL) was acquired by Westcliff, the reverse of 1952 and this company passed to the MBO. It was agreed by NBC and the Ministry of Transport, that as the MBO were acquiring the goodwill generated by the name Eastern National over the years, that the new owners could change the name of the Westcliff company to Eastern National Ltd, and trade as 'Eastern National'.

However, when Westcliff applied to change the name to Eastern National Ltd, Companies House objected as their rules forbade the use of 'National' in a new company name unless it was genuinely National. It took ministerial discussions between Transport and Trade departments to allow the MBO to use the name it thought it had bought! Circle completed!

ENL was acquired by Badgerline Holdings Ltd on 12 April 1990. Badgerline were in favour of smaller operating units to enable greater management focus, so the South Essex and London operations were transferred to another new company Thamesway Ltd in July 1990, covering the area served by the original Westcliff-on-Sea Motor Services Ltd in 1951, ENL serving the area of the original ENOC at the same date.

Another circle was completed.

Badgerline was also keen that its success with high frequency commercial minibus operation was extended to its new acquisitions. Such services were uncommon with Eastern National, apart from one in Clacton and Brentwood town services, and for one route in Chelmsford.

Ford Transits arrived from City Line and Badgerline with Thamesway in Southend in large numbers supplemented by large fleets of new Mercedes 709Ds in a competitive foray against municipally owned Southend Transport in 1991. Eastern National received similar vehicles for use in Bishops Stortford, Braintree, Chelmsford, Maldon and Witham

In 1993 second hand 608Ds arrived from sister Badgerline Group companies to enable a competitive strike by Eastern National on Colchester Borough Transport. Both Southend and Colchester 'Bus Wars' (as the media like to call them) were ended, in 1993 and 1994 respectively. The Competition Authorities permitted in each case coordination agreements to return for one day only, with agreed timetables being submitted to the Traffic Commissioners on the same day. Two circles closed for one day!

This division of Thamesway and Eastern National remained until 1996, when First Group (formed from a merger of Badgerline and GRT groups in 1995) decided to merge Eastern National and Thamesway as one company (another circle closed!). To demonstrate that this was a merger, not a takeover of Thamesway by ENL, it was decided to rename Eastern National Ltd as Essex Buses Ltd, trading under the two separate fleetnames and liveries.

But those are not the only circles. Eastern National's history began in 1909 with the start of the National Steam Car Company, started by one Thomas Clarkson, to operate Clarkson's steam buses which he built in Chelmsford. The last Managing Director of ENOC as a bus operator in 1986 was one (unrelated) Geoffrey Clarkson! Both were Lancastrians, though!

Add to that that current owner First Group in 1997 acquired two rail franchises, Great Eastern, covering part of ENOC's old shareholder LNER, and the Great Western Railway.

I cannot help but muse on the changes to the industry which will come following the Covid-19 pandemic. Nothing is really new and more circles will be closed, but I am sure that the wheels on the bus will continue to go round and round.

RO

Perhaps the last ENOC bus to bear the Eastern National fleetname. No. 654, T654 SSF, Scania L, pictured here in First Bus livery on Service 65A at Colchester High Street in 2001.

ENOC bus type Leyland TS1 travels south along Chelmsford High Street in 1930. The Shire Hall is in the background which dates from 1789–91 and is extant.

A very busy scene at the original site of the ENOC Chelmsford Bus Station, Christmas 1931. It might have been Christmas Eve with the number of people about, but there do not appear to be many buses to take them all home.

EASTERN NATIONAL

Associated with the L.M.S. and L.N.E. Railways

Service No. 43.

BRENTWOOD—BILLERICAY

EXTENSION OF ROUTE
TO AND FROM STOCK

WITH REVISED TIME TABLE AS FROM

SATURDAY, MAY 14th, 1938

Service No. 43.   BRENTWOOD-HUTTON-BILLERICAY-STOCK.

Saturdays.

		p.m.	p.m.	p.m.	p.m.	p.m.	p.m.	p.m.	Thro' Fare
Brentwood, Yorkshire Grey	dep.	2 31	3 31	4 31	5 31	7 31	8 31	9 31	Fare
Shenfield, Green Dragon		2 34	3 34	4 34	5 34	7 34	8 34	9 34	1d
Hutton, The Chequers		2 42	3 42	4 42	5 42	7 42	8 42	9 42	3d
Billericay, High Street		2 51	3 51	4 51	5 51	7 51	8 51	9 51	5d
Stock, The Bear	arr.	3 0		5 0		8 0	9 0		9d

		p.m.	p.m.	p.m.	p.m.	p.m.	p.m.	p.m.	Thro' Fare
Stock, The Bear	dep.	3 1		5 1		8 1	9 1		Fare
Billericay, High Street		3 10	4 10	5 10	6 10	8 10	9 10	1010	4d
Hutton, The Chequers		3 19	4 19	5 19	6 19	8 19	9 19	1019	6d
Shenfield, Green Dragon		3 27	4 27	5 27	6 27	8 27	9 27	1027	8d
Brentwood, Yorkshire Grey	arr.	3 30	4 30	5 30	6 30	8 30	9 30	1030	9d

Sundays.

		p.m.	p.m.	p.m.	p.m.	Thro' Fare
Brentwood, Yorkshire Grey	dep.	2 31	3 31	4 31	5 31	Fare
Shenfield, Green Dragon		2 34	3 34	4 34	5 34	1d
Hutton, The Chequers		2 42	3 42	4 42	5 42	3d
Billericay, High Street		2 51	3 51	4 51	5 51	5d
Stock, The Bear	arr.					

		p.m.	p.m.	p.m.	p.m.	p.m.	Thro' Fare
Stock, The Bear	dep.						Fare
Billericay, High Street		3 10	4 10	5 10	6 10	8 10	—
Hutton, The Chequers		3 19	4 19	5 19	6 19	8 19	2d
Shenfield, Green Dragon		3 27	4 27	5 27	6 27	8 27	4d
Brentwood, Yorkshire Grey	arr.	3 30	4 30	5 30	6 30	8 30	5d

Return Fares.

Brentwood, Yorkshire Grey-Billericay	8d	Shenfield, Green Dragon-Billericay	6d
Brentwood, Yorkshire Grey-Hart's Corner	6d	Stock, The Bear-Billericay	7d

A Reminder ! DAILY COACH SERVICE TO

ROMFORD, ILFORD, STRATFORD & LONDON (Bow)

From SHENFIELD (Green Dragon) : At 11 and 41 minutes past each hour from 6.41 a.m. to 10.41 p.m. (from 7.41 a.m. on Sundays).

From BRENTWOOD (Yorkshire Grey) : At 15 and 45 minutes past each hour from 6.45 a.m. to 10.45 p.m. (from 7.45 a.m. on Sundays).

FARES TO LONDON (Bow)—From Shenfield ... ... 1/4 Single ; 2/2 Return
From Brentwood ... ... 1/3 Single ; 2/- Return

COMPANY REGULATIONS —Passengers are conveyed subject to the advertised conditions contained in the current official Time Table Booklets.

THE EASTERN NATIONAL OMNIBUS CO., LTD.,

Head Offices : NEW WRITTLE STREET, CHELMSFORD

Phone : 3431 (3 lines)

Local Offices :
OMNIBUS STATION
CHELMSFORD
'Phone : 3104

Local Offices :
BADDOW ROAD CORNER
ENQUIRY OFFICE
CHELMSFORD

EN. AD. 3731/438   2M.

ENOC publicity leaflet for Service 43. This service was in direct competition with the City Coach Company Ltd. who operated services between Brentwood and Billericay including their historic Route 1 between London (Wood Green) and Southend-on-Sea which had a frequency of every 15 minutes. Needless to say ENOC curtailed the route at Billericay from 30th March, 1939 before it was abandoned in the October of that year.

Clockwise from top left: A busy post-war scene at Bedford Bus Station. In view is ENOC No 3932, LPU 622, Bedford OB which had a Perkins P6 oil engine. It passed to the United Counties Omnibus Co. Ltd in 1952 before becoming service lorry No 39 in 1954.

Helping out at Aylesbury. ENOC Bus No 3153 TM 9185, Leyland TD1. New to ENOC in 1931 for use on an abortive tramway replacement scheme at Luton. You may observe the advert for Wenleys Ltd at Chelmsford which suggests 3153 had already moved to Chelmsford.

A quiet wartime scene at Bedford Bus Station. A splendid ENOC line up in ths view from left to right: No 3753 GNO 697 Bristol K5G, No 3415 AEV 785 Dennis Lancet, No 3078 TM 8194 AEC Regent, No 3744 GNO 688 Bristol K5G. Photo © J.F. Parke

Wartime at Harrold ENOC Bus No 2824, TM 4159, Leyland PLSC3 on Service 6 to Bedford via Felmersham and Milton Ernest. Behind is Birch Bros, BLO 977.

Memories – Off the buses at Head Office and Depots

Firstly in 1950 …

Looking back, I joined EN as a "sprog" traffic clerk in September 1950 (EN was then only 20 years old, but already it had come a long way). So in 1950 it was time to leave school. The teachers at Northgate Grammar School in Ipswich were trying to get me into the various occupations that they knew about, but I was somewhat determined to get into the bus industry. They were horrified! So I was on my own with making applications!

Having tried Eastern Counties Bus Company in Ipswich without success, I was fortunate to become a Traffic Clerk at Eastern National at their Head Office in Chelmsford. This meant going into lodgings ("digs" as they were commonly known in those days), and I found these outside Chelmsford at Boyton Cross, Roxwell. Now, for a "townie" this was a culture shock. Water from a pump from goodness knows where, and the toilet down the garden! A double seat! Some Ipswich neighbours came to the rescue, and I moved back into Chelmsford, with a family. This was at Springfield Park, with a big wall at the bottom of the garden to protect us from the inmates of Chelmsford Prison. So began for real "my life on the buses". This was now September 1950.

I worked in the Traffic Department Publicity Section at New Writtle Street, (Head Office), which had been there since 1932, when the company moved there from Brompton Road, London. I worked alongside Donald MacGregor, who later became Managing Director of Hedingham Omnibuses. Our job was to write up 'copy' for time and fare tables, excursions and express service leaflets, checking the printers' proofs, and arranging the distribution. In charge of us was Fred Spindler, who had originated at Brompton Road.

However, much as I was enjoying the work, the wages for a young lad (£2 pw) only covered lodgings from Monday to Friday, and my parents were paying the rail fare home on Saturday for the weekend (it was, of course, a 5½ day week at the time). My personal pride told me I couldn't let them keep this up, so I tried for a job with a local coach company in Ipswich, P & M Coach Lines, who were gaining a reputation with holiday tours. I was successful, and handed in my notice to Eastern National. Then a problem at the last minute; P&M said there was to be a delay – they didn't say how long, or why. But the die was cast, and personal pride took over again. Through a friend, I managed to get a job in the Publicity Department at Ransomes Sims & Jeffries, the agricultural firm, in Ipswich.

However, RS&J turned out to be something of a "sweatshop", even for clerical staff, and luckily after 5 weeks P&M said they could accept me. But my 6-week sojourn out of the bus industry convinced me that that was where I wanted to be! I joined P&M at £2.10 a week (£2.50 new money)!

Moving forward to the 80's and 90's …. *(After 6 years with P&M,(including 2 years RAF National Service) I spent 18 years at East Kent, then 4½. years at National Travel South East, I transferred to Eastern National at Chelmsford from NTSE as Coaching Manager on 1 October 1978, following the National Bus Company's decision to return coach operations to the bus companies.*

In 1980, the licensing restrictions on coach work were lifted, and I devised the Highwayman cross-country network of routes. During the summer, the Saturday only routes of National Express to the East, South coast and South West were taken over as domestic Highwayman Holiday routes, continuing the interchange at Basildon. We also started the Leisure Break Holiday**s** (a title now copied by other holiday companies and hotels). These were short duration tours of 3–4 days, which wouldn't compromise the National Holiday tours, which we also operated under contract.

At the same time, we were operating some coaches on contract to National Express, which by now had become a separate entity.

On 14 February 1983 bespoke commuter services started jointly with Grey Green from Essex to London; GG withdrew from the EAX Pool on 25 February 1985; EN/GG took over Tellyn's Commuter Coach operations from Witham in February 1988; in March 1990, intervention by the OFT necessitated the Commuter Pool Agreement to be terminated; in January 1999 EN withdrew its operations.

In 1985, EN was gearing itself up for privatisation of the National Bus Company. Preparations were being made for a new management structure. I was given the task of managing the Braintree, Uttlesford & East Herts District. All the district managers' areas were allied to the local authority areas, in order to be able to maintain closer contact with them under the new forthcoming freedom from licensing regime.

An important feature of my area was the development of Stansted Airport as London's third airport. Contact was maintained with its management team to ensure mutual advantage for passengers and its staff.

In May 1986 the first Minibus operations were introduced – "Coastline", whilst through 1985/96, we were developing our LRT contracts. And, of course, we had to prepare ourselves for 26 October 1986 – Deregulation of Bus Services. A "commercial network" of services was registered with the Traffic Commissioners. This represented about 80% of the Companies' previous commercial mileage. A significant new commercial service introduction for my area was the daily 333 from Stansted Airport to Bishops Stortford, Harlow, Epping and Loughton.

So progress towards privatisation was being made through 1986. A Management Buy-Out was being prepared – I was one of the seven area managers who became minor shareholders in the new company, with four major shareholders – the General Manager, Finance Manager, Operations Manager and Fleet Engineer. Privatisation eventually took place on 23 December 1986 So we developed the newly-privatised company, with many new services, some lower fares – minibuses were tried – and found to be successful with higher frequencies and lower costs.

In January 1987 I was asked to return to Head Office as Manager, Contracts & Commercial Activities, and apart from marketing, I was also involved with administration of the London Transport contracts which we had been successful in obtaining. During this time, I took over the responsibility for the Printing Department at Eastern National. This was

ENOC dual purpose bus No 4509, B697 BPU, Leyland Olympian. In use on service 53, Chelmsford–Colchester and subsequently on Braintree–London commuter services.

ENOC dual purpose bus No 1111 HHJ 372Y. Leyland Tiger Route branded for the London Stansted Airport Rail Air Link and seen at the old terminal in 1983.

an in-house unit, which had achieved considerable recognition throughout National Bus Company. My responsibilities also included the Roadside Publicity staff, who looked after bus stops and roadside timetables.

Eastern National became more successful, and in July 1990 we joined the Badgerline Group (another privatised group out of NBC). I became the company's Marketing Manager, mostly doing the same things as before. This position I held until my early retirement in 1996. A particularly interesting responsibility was as Editor of *"The Grapevine"*, a bi-monthly news magazine about EN, mainly for its staff, but widely read outside the company! EN had been involved with Stansted Airport management over a number of years on the provision of bus services as the airport was developing. Consequently when HM The Queen officially opened the futuristic £400m New Terminal on 15 March 1991, I was invited to represent EN.

I was due to retire in 1999 and in various discussions the company's Director of Operations offered an early retirement and I retired on 30 April 1996 at age 62 to be able to enjoy life for my later years!

I retained an interest at Eastern National, in that I continued to look after the company's archives. In view of the company's move from New Writtle Street to Westway in October 2004. I completed the boxing up of all the archives and transferred them to the Essex Records Office. And just as I had written the 60 Year book about the company, so I was also involved with the 75 Years book

Right: Grays in 1951. ENOC, bus no. 3929, LPU 619, Bedford OB with a heavy load for Blackshotts Lane on Service 32B. On 30th September in the same year this service and all local services would pass to the London Transport Executive who took over the operation of ENOC's garage in Argent Street, Grays. ENOC would be left with long-distance services to and from Grays and Tilbury Ferry with various destinations throughout Essex including Brentwood, Chelmsford, Clacton-on-Sea and Southend-on-Sea.

I have served in 6 types of company:

In a Tilling (nationalised (BTC) company: 1950–51 (almost 1 year)
(Difficult to realise that EN was then only 2 years into nationalisation)

In a privately-owned company: 1951–56 (5 years)

In a BET (private multiple) company: 1956–69 (13 years)

In an NBC (nationalised) company(ies) (3)   1969–86 (17 years)

In a privately-owned company (as a Shareholder)   1986–90 (4 years)

(and part of the Management Buyout Team)

In a privately-owned Group company (2):   1990–96 (6 years)

Total: 46 years

(but Long Service only counts from 1956)

GD

Happy Days – Mostly!

I joined Eastern National on 4th January 1965, having spent nearly two years with George Ewer and Co (Grey Green).

I was allocated to the Publicity team, lead by Fred Spindler. After a short while, it was on to Road Service Licensing with Eric Farage in charge. We worked in the office overlooking one end of Central Works and the steam cleaning facility so saw vehicles which were coming into CW for major docking. Bob Beaumont, Peter Stobart, Tony Spindler and myself made up the Licensing section.

Next it was to a newly created Special Duties under Mike Merton. The paths of Mike and I met many times over the years, culminating in us working together at Essex County Council and, in 1994, me taking over from him as Passenger Transport Manager. Special Duties encompassed a range of functions, most of them away from New Writtle Street, including mileaging of new and revised services, service investigation and a bit of liaison with local authorities. After a short while, to make space at HO, we were outstationed to a spare office at Duke Street where we were made very welcome by the local staff (it might have been because if they were a bit pushed, Mike and I would help them out on the phone, travel office or whatever)

I then went back to HO where I joined Peter Dobson in the General traffic office, which mainly dealt with Fares and Recruitment issues.

However, my time at Duke Street had whetted my appetite for depot work as I saw this being where things really happened and when the chance to return to Duke Street as Traffic Assistant came up, I took it with both hands. It gave me my first experience of dealing with (minor) staff matters under the guidance of Arthur Allen. Arthur was the Assistant District Traffic Superintendent and was a great tutor for there was nothing he hadn't seen before and so didn't get excited. In overall charge was Stan Lewis who, like Arthur, was a true busman having started out with Westcliff Motor Services (he may have also been Benfleet and District but

I am not sure about that). Stan was also unflappable and he only vented his feelings when there was an impracticable instruction issued from Head Office!

I got hauled back to HO for a while to re-join the Licensing section when they were a bit short staffed but in 1971, became Assistant DTS at Basildon, working for a great boss, Ken Cox. Another proper busman, Ken was ex City. Basildon and Chelmsford Depots were chalk and cheese. Chelmsford was predominately crew operation, long standing staff, many crews being husband driving and wife conducting (it always intrigued me what they found to talk about, working and living together) whereas Basildon had a very high turnover of staff and had much more OMO. Although they had their moments, Basildon staff were much more willing to adjust their way of working – provided it ensured higher earnings as living in Basildon wasn't cheap.

Basildon was noted for its high staff shortage (the much higher pay just up the road at LT Hornchurch and Romford garages tempted many) and so I typically spent a day and a half to two days a week interviewing prospective road staff, just to keep up with the rate of people leaving. I was also given the job of dealing with most disciplinary matters although generally, if it looked like someone was for the chop, Ken handled it. I certainly did not enjoy this aspect of the job; too often I could see myself in the shoes of the member of staff sitting in front of me and yet I had to take action – most of this was for poor attendance, a problem exacerbated by the long hours most were working to make ends meet and tiredness took its toll.

After two years at Basildon, when Doug Flack was moved from Traffic Superintendent at Brentwood to the same role at Wood Green, I was sent to Brentwood, still under Ken Cox. Brentwood shared the staff shortage problem, with the two LT Romford garages six miles away. What was different though was that it did have quite a few long serving staff, ex City. Brentwood was an interesting experience. In many ways, there were three quite separate operations. There was the local (crew) rota, the OMO rota (quite small) and the Main Road rota. This was the 'pecking' order.

New staff started on Locals, and if a vacancy arose could apply for OMO or Main Road. The strange thing was that having started out on local services, once they became 'Main Road' staff, even if we were short, they couldn't be used to fill in on local services!

And so, after a year at Brentwood, in July 1974 I went to work for Essex County Council, intending to go for a couple of years and then back to the operating industry. It didn't work out like that and 31 years later, I retired from ECC. Happy days (mostly) at ENOC.

DW

The top picture of Brentwood High Street looking further east towards the traffic signal junction known as Wilson's Corner named after the large store in Ingrave Road, (A128); ENOC Bus No. 119, HVW 214, Leyland TEC2 GNU (ex City Coach Company Ltd. and bearing Westcliff-on-Sea fleet names) awaits departure to London (Wood Green) in 1955. The picture below shows the Eastern National and Westcliff-on-Sea Enquiry and Booking Office at 3 High Street which was virtually opposite the bus stop for Wood Green; the editor was a frequent caller to purchase London Transport 'Red Rover' and express coach tickets.

Two pictures of Brentwood High Street in the 1950s are all before DW arrived at Brentwood Depot, although the services to Romford and Tilbury Ferry would remain throughout his tenure in 1973/4. The top picture shows ENOC Bus No. 1136, FJN 204, Leyland PD2/12 (ex Westcliff-on-Sea Motor Services) awaiting departure for Romford on Service 30 in 1957. The bottom picture shows ENOC dual purpose Bus No. 297, MPU 31, Bristol L5G at the same bus stop bound for Tilbury Ferry on Service 40 in 1954. Brentwood High Street has seen many changes since then with the Yorkshire Grey P.H. on the left side of the road now demolished, however the concrete block in front of the P.H. contains public toilets below road level and is extant.

A brief stay at Chelmsford

One thing I was sure of as I prepared to leave school was that I wanted to work for a bus company so imagine my joy at finding a small ad in the Essex Chronicle announcing 'Traffic Clerks wanted for interesting duties in the Traffic Department of the Eastern National Omnibus Company Ltd based at New Writtle Street Chelmsford. Apply to J Wilson, Assistant Traffic Manager (Commercial). I was interviewed on Saturday March 2nd 1964 and was infected with John Wilson's enthusiasm so I was delighted when I got one of the jobs and started on August 19 at a wage of £6.11.0 per week.

I had been allocated to the Licencing Office located in a corner position on the first floor of the then modern Head Office building, a room that I shared with Eric Farage (Ref 3 /5 (for Licencing Section)), universally known as Frisky because he wasn't, Bob Beaumont (3/5A) who was my supervisor, and Gerald Searle (3/5B), a brilliant designer who was later responsible for the Eastern National logo. 3 covered the Traffic department, and 5, the Licencing department. Hours of work were 0845 to 1730 Monday to Friday with a lunch break from 1250 to 1350. Signing in and out was required, which revealed my frequent late arrivals. My pay number was T57 and my telephone number was Chelmsford 3431 extn 64.

As the junior, my duties were obviously going to be less interesting than everybody else and revolved around the publication of Notices and Proceedings for all the Traffic Areas. In them were published every application to apply for a new, or vary an existing, road service licence as well as fares applications and objections from competing operators. For the Eastern and Metropolitan Traffic Areas, all pages had to be closely examined in case we needed to object to someone else's application. After due process, sometimes involving a public sitting, the Traffic Commissioner would either grant the application as applied for or with modification or refuse it completely. Some routes which visited more than one Traffic Area required backing licences for each. Here the extensive EN

Extended Tour programme was something of a curse and it got to the stage where I knew by heart many of the routes and I still remember gems such as `unclassified road via Drumnadrochit`

The job was made easier because Mr Farage always went through the N&P`s as they arrived and marked the relevant entries; he never missed anything. All of the stage carriage applications were entered against the licence concerned on an enormous ledger (nowadays it would be called a spreadsheet) and their progress through the system was diligently recorded; my main task was to keep this up-to date.

I was living at Barkingside at the time and travelled on my staff pass changing at Brentwood, often in the company of a very young Andy Gipson. This meant leaving home at 0700 and returning just after 1900. Anyway time passed agreeably enough and all three of my colleagues were very easy going and tolerant of my many shortcomings. I was able to tap in to their wisdom and experience and eventually I was able to work the Banda machine without covering myself in purple ink. Above all, I formed a lifelong friendship with Bob Beaumont and we shared the ups and downs of our lives. I also got to know the residents of other departments such as Jim Cressey, who later joined National Express, Roger Bowker who went on to greatness with Stagecoach, David Domin, who rode a motor bike and was late nearly as often as I was plus many others including Ray Boreham, Michael Pleasants, John Dowsett and Terry Smith, who with many others combined to make Eastern National Head Office an efficient but happy workplace.

Nine months rolled by before John Wilson gave me a bit of career counselling (or perhaps he just wanted to get rid of me) as a result of which I departed for the sharp end of the business, reporting to Inspector Kennedy at the Southend Conductor Training School on Monday June 22 1964, but that is another story.

BB

1956–1959 at Head Office

In the last term of my fifth year at Westcliff High School, I had the usual interview with the careers' master, Mr Harden, who also happened to be my Latin master. Interestingly, I cannot remember ever being told that if you stayed on to the sixth form there was the possibility of going to university. Anyway, I was determined to leave school and, if possible, work in the transport industry, preferably with Eastern National. As a result, Mr Harden arranged for me to have an interview with Mr. Frank Bryan, the Traffic Manager of Eastern National. This interview duly took place at the Southend Offices of Eastern National. Mr Bryan was, of course, based at the New Writtle Street, Head Office of Eastern National, in Chelmsford.

I cannot remember exactly what I said at this interview but I must have said something about an interest in schedules and timetables. (Incidentally in my high school years I had 'run' an imaginary bus called 'South Essex' complete with timetables for local and long-distance services. I had worked out the vehicle workings and so on, and also had a fleet list! I did not tell Mr Bryan about this!). Anyway, at the beginning of September 1956, I reported to the Eastern National Head Office at New Writtle Street, Chelmsford.

The journey to Chelmsford involved two buses. The No. 1 from Hadleigh to Rayleigh, worked by Southend Corporation, and then a No.11, worked by Southend Garage, or 11A (the Direct Service), worked by Chelmsford Garage, from Rayleigh to Chelmsford. I travelled on the 7.21am from Hadleigh and caught the 7.55am (11) or the 8am (11A) from Rayleigh. Fortunately on the first day that I started work, I was given a Privilege Ticket which gave me free travel to and from work and half-fare at other times. During holidays we were given free Privilege Tickets for the duration of the holiday. It all seems a bit mean compared with the concessions that bus company employees receive these days!

Bus-wise the journey from Hadleigh to Rayleigh was usually by an AEC Regent III, although on occasions it was an AEC Regent I or a Daimler

CVA6 or CVD6. A year or so later, Leyland PD2s from the second batch (287 – 298) appeared on the No. 1 service as they had slightly lower bodies than the first batch and were thus able to work under Hockley Railway Bridge on Service 7 to which the No 1 vehicles changed at Rayleigh. All, of course, had the standard (for Southend Corporation) Massey low-bridge body. (Although a batch of PD2/20s with Weymann Orion bodies – 299–304 – appeared later on this route). The journey from Rayleigh to Chelmsford was, invariably, by Bristol KSW5G. Lodekkas had not yet graduated to these workings. The Chelmsford buses always seemed to be better turned out than the Southend ones: no doubt it had something to do with being nearer Head Office. However the Southend buses always seemed faster than buses at most EN Garages except Hadleigh! The Chief Engineer probably kept a close eye on how well the engines of the Chelmsford vehicles were governed. And the Southend vehicles probably had a harder life than those at most other garages.

On the first day at work I soon discovered that there were a number of other young people employed at EN Head Office who travelled on the Service 11/11A from Battlesbridge and Rettendon and we travelled together on the 11A service.

In the evenings there were buses from Chelmsford to Rayleigh (and onwards to Southend) at 5.35pm (11A), worked by Southend Garage, and 5.40pm (11), worked by Chelmsford Garage. Perhaps I should explain that the normal service, No.11, travelled via East Hanningfield and usually left Chelmsford at forty minutes past each hour whereas the 11A travelled direct via the Main Road from Howe Green to Rettendon "Bell". At that time, the Service 11A was a relatively new innovation and there were only two or three journeys each day. Service 11 was hourly.

I reported for work on my first day at New Writtle Street and was given my pay-roll number which was T49: 'T' stood for traffic. All office staff had to sign in everyday at a machine. I cannot remember if we had to sign out. My starting pay at the age of sixteen was £3.10 shillings (£3.50p) for a five and a half day week. The Traffic Department was under the immediate control of the Traffic Assistant Mr. Hanley. His own section seemed to deal with policy matters and fares. There was also the licensing section under Mr. Farage and the Publicity Section under Mr. Spindler.

I was introduced to the Schedules Section in the Traffic Office. My interest in Schedules must have been apparent to Mr. Bryan the Traffic Manager. The head of the Schedules Section was Charlie English and there were six other members of the section each of whom had responsibilities for one garage or a group of garages: Ron Holmes for Chelmsford, Chris Gibbs for Clacton, Dovercourt and Walton, Stan Chamberlain for Colchester and West Mersea, Geoff Goodwin for Braintree and Halstead, Ray Hodges for the 251 and John Hales for Brentwood Locals. I cannot remember who was responsible for Maldon and Bishops Stortford. Sometime later we were joined by Ken Branch who lived in Basildon and after a while took charge of the, at that time, rapidly expanding Basildon Garage.

My first job was to assist Ray Hodges and copy Service 251 car (vehicle) and crew "horizontal" graphs. I soon got the hang of how to read them and found them very interesting. The journeys that each car and crew worked could be clearly seen and it was also possible to see where there were gaps into which extra journeys could be fitted. I later worked with vertical, or "up and down", graphs as a timing clerk at British Railways.

Service 251 was treated as an entity in itself. The "cars" used to work it were divided between the three garages involved: that is Southend Tylers Avenue, Brentwood and Wood Green. This meant that some vehicles did not return to their own garage each night and that crews worked vehicles from other garages. I cannot remember how many vehicles were allocated to this long (47 miles) and intense (every 15 minutes) service but the service vehicles alone must have accounted for 24.

There were also many duplicate vehicles scheduled. And there were some not shown on the main graphs: my eldest brother, who was at Hadleigh Garage by this time, told me of a 251 duplicate that he had worked from Wickford to Rayleigh with a Bedford/Beadle chassis-less single-decker. His main comment was that the cab was very hot on a summer's day! I also remember overhearing some of the hierarchy in the Traffic and Schedules Section discussing workings on which these vehicles could be used as the

Chief Engineer had pointed out that they were more economical fuel-wise – they had by now been fitted with Gardner 4LK engines. This may have been during the Suez Crisis when oil supplies we were disrupted.

Back to the 251, I am not sure which vehicles were working this service at the time but I do know that some of the "City" Leyland PD1s had been moved to Hadleigh Garage as I had travelled on a Roberts-bodied one on Service 3. Bristol Lodekkas were introduced in large numbers commencing with the DHK (suffix) LD5Gs in 1955. After a relatively short time, it became clear that these 5LW engined vehicles were not suitable for this long and demanding route and Bristol engined LD6Bs were introduced as they became available. However the six Leyland bodied PD2/12s which had been ordered by "City" remained on the 251 taking their turn alongside the Lodekkas.

After some months it must have become clear that I had an aptitude for schedules and I was allowed to do the schedules for some small garages for Bank Holiday workings. Besides drawing the graphs and planning the car and crew workings, the schedules clerks also had to write up the crew workings so that the crews could take them on the road and work the relevant journeys. They were a bit like this: if my memory serves me right!

Maldon Garage: Tuesdays and Fridays						
Car no.	Time	From	To	Service	Running time mins	Stand time mins
	7.00 am	Sign on				10
MN3	7.10 am	Car to Stand				
	7.15 am	Maldon	Chelmsford	31	43	2
	8.00 am	Chelmsford	Maldon	31	43	2
	8.45 am	Maldon	Chelmsford	31	43	2
	9.30 am	Chelmsford	Maldon	31	43	2
	10.13 am	Park bus for 10.15 am service 31				
	10.15 am	Off duty				
	11.10 am	On duty, take over bus				
MN5	11.15 am	Maldon	Burnham on Crouch	91	48	7
	12.10 pm	Burnham on Crouch	Maldon	91	48	
	12.58 pm	Car to Garage				2
	1.00 pm	Spare duty				35
SD12	1.35 pm	Car to Stand				
	1.40 pm	Maldon	Goldhanger	95	19	1
	2.00 pm	Goldhanger	Maldon via Heybridge Basin	94	24	
	2.24 pm	Park bus				
	2.45 pm	Maldon	Heybridge Basin	94	12	3
	3.00 pm	Heybridge Basin	Maldon	94	12	
	3.12 pm	Park bus for service 96 to Woodham Ferrers				
	3.12 pm	Sign off				10
	3.22 pm	Off duty.				

This is as near as my memory will allow me to replicate a typical duty. These duties were written up on "Banda" spirit duplicator ink-sheets. It was a messy process. The permanent duties were typed for longevity and clarity. There was also a column on each duty which showed the mileage covered by each journey. At the bottom of the duty sheet there was a summary of the hours worked, spread-over and total mileage. When a Maldon crew took over a car from another garage on services 19/19A it was shown as SD Car (Southend), CN Car (Clacton) or CO Car (Colchester). Maldon Garage itself put out one car onto the 19/19A Services and worked Maldon to Southend and Maldon to Colchester. Southend crews usually worked Southend to Colchester and back. Colchester crews worked Colchester to Southend and back and also Colchester to Clacton and return. Thus, Colchester crews were the only ones that worked the whole length of the routes. The Southend crews had a 12 minute turn-round at Colchester having worked from Southend for 2 hours and 23minutes and Colchester had 4(!) minutes at Southend after a journey of the same length. Clacton crews only worked the 19and 19A between Clacton and Colchester. All four garages put out cars on these routes.

The reason that I have given an example from Maldon Garage is because after a year or so I was given responsibility for Maldon and Bishops Stortford Garages under the supervision of Charlie English. Both were interesting in their own way. Both had services that worked into Chelmsford: Maldon on the 31 and the 37 (via Woodham Walter) and Bishops Stortford on the 58. Maldon usually put out a Lodekka and two Bristol KSWs on the 31 and an L5G on the 37 (which only ran on Wednesdays, Fridays & Saturdays). Maldon also worked routes to Braintree (335) and Bradwell-on-Sea and Burnham-on-Crouch.

It was at the time that the Bradwell Nuclear Power Station was being built and on Saturdays the Maldon Bradwell (92) late night service was duplicated by a double-decker: the service car was a Bristol SC one-person operated vehicle. We found out this piece of interesting information purely by chance. The duplicate car was never officially scheduled. This is a good example of the relationship between the schedules section at Chelmsford. Almost all communication was by company post, the relevant District

Traffic Superintendent or an occasional telephone call. The District Traffic Superintendents jealously guarded their kingdoms. There were four District Traffic Superintendents at that time: one at Chelmsford, Clacton who covered Dovercourt, Colchester and Halstead as well, Southend with whom we had little to do, and one who had responsibility for the rest of the garages which were mainly in the rural area (such as Maldon and Bishops Stortford).

The impression that I got was that it would not be appropriate for a lowly schedules clerk to be involved too closely with the garage for which he prepared the schedules. I do not think that it would have been considered a good use of manpower and company resources to allow us to spend a day visiting the garages with which we were concerned and, perhaps, riding on some of the routes involved. In other organisations it would probably be regarded as of good educational value and an encouragement to the workers.

The fact is that most of the schedules clerks only saw the garages with which they were concerned in their own time when passing through the town concerned. While I knew Maldon and its environs, I never visited Bishops Stortford. Looking back with the benefit hindsight, and a certain amount of maturity and experience, I can see that it would have been all too easy for an outsider from Head Office to upset the delicate balance that existed between the management and the trade unions. However, it would have done no harm if we had been given a pass for the day and told to go and ride on some of the routes worked by the garage for which we were responsible incognito. There is also the fact that Eastern National was run on very frugal lines: operationally and engineering-wise. Having said that, I have no doubt that it made a profit and you rarely saw one of its buses a failure on the road!

Bishops Stortford Garage also worked routes some way from home. The main routes were the 58 (to Chelmsford, on which it put out KSWs), the 301 (Bishops Stortford to Saffron Walden) and the 338 (Bishops Stortford to Thaxted). The 338 was a railway replacement service to cover the closure of the Elsenham to Thaxted branch line (it was introduced as the

38 on 15/9/52 and renumbered to 338 in 1955 and then to 302 in 1968). There were also forays to the south and east of Bishops Stortford to places like Dunmow (310 duplicates), to Ongar (33A) and to Harlow on the 46 and 47. The 46 also operated to Chelmsford. Most of these services were operated by one person operators using Bristol SC buses.

In my late childhood the nationalisation of the transport system was taking place under the Attlee government. This was something that as a child and teenager I fully agreed with and I still believe that there should be a high degree of public ownership, or at least control, if we are to ever have a good system of public transport. Anyway, I went to work at Eastern National as a naive teenager thinking that I would be working for a nationalised transport company. Of course it was nationalised: Eastern National was part of the Tilling Group which had been nationalised. However it seemed to me that it was not nationalised. As far as I could see, it was still run as a private Tilling Group company. Every other operator was treated as a rival. London Transport and British Railways were in the same camp as Moores of Kelvedon and Osbornes of Tollesbury, as far Eastern National were concerned!

One incident sticks in my mind. The Traffic Assistant's section wanted to know what the wording was on London Transport's RFs that warned people not to stand by the driver. The clerk in the Traffic Assistant's section was sent to ride on an RF somewhere so as to find out!

During the 1958 bus strike it was realised that I would not be able to get to work at Chelmsford and thus I was told to report to the Southend office. Eastern National crews were on strike but Southend Corporation crews were still working. Rather than risk not getting on a Corporation bus as there were only two each hour each way (four in the peak) between Hadleigh and Southend for most of the day, I cycled to and from Southend. For me this experience was a real treat. For a week, at least, I would be working in the office that scheduled the buses that ran in my local area.

Southend Garage and Office scheduled its own buses and crews and also those of Hadleigh and Canvey Garages, except of course, for Southend

Tylers Avenue. I was made very welcome by Gerry Neville, the Schedules Clerk, and given some general schedules work to do, such as copying graphs and writing up duties. It was a very enjoyable week. I was interested to note that the actual vehicle number for each car working was pencilled in at the side of the working. In the schedules that we prepared, we just scheduled the workings and it was up to the garage concerned to decide which actual vehicle was allocated to that particular car duty.

In May 1957, the new Central Works of Eastern National was opened. This was a big event and the office staff was allowed to use part of the canteen. This meant that we could see into the works and see what vehicles were receiving attention. The thing that struck me was the thoroughness with which the overhauls were carried out. Even pre-war vehicles were stripped down, refurbished and sent out as though they were new buses. There can be few operators these days that can still overhaul buses to such a high standard. Living in Blackpool now, I do know that Blackpool Transport continues to do such work on buses and trams. One indication of the care that was taken at the works with the presentation of the buses was that before brand new buses were put into service; the black band which separated the cream from the green on the body was re-painted dark green.

Occasionally I had the opportunity to see files about services and this was very interesting and informative. However the sight of such files was frowned upon unless we had a direct need to see them. On one occasion I happened to see the records for the Lodekka (LD5G) based at Walton-on-Naze (I think it was 214 BPU). The astonishing thing was that it was returning 17 miles per gallon: not bad for a 58-seat double-decker! What bus companies would give for such economy today: even in the 1950s, Eastern National was doing its bit for the environment!

Having said that Eastern National was run on frugal lines, there were occasional treats for the staff. One was in 1958 when a group of us made a Saturday visit to Eastern Coach Works at Lowestoft. We travelled on a Chelmsford Bristol L6B with ECW "Queen Mary" body and were treated to lunch at an inn in Lowestoft. The visit was very interesting because we were able to see how the bodies were constructed and inspect vehicles destined for various parts of the United Kingdom including some LD6Gs for the Scottish Bus Group. They looked very nice in their very different liveries: different, that is, to the standard Tilling livery.

Earlier on, I mentioned that one of the reasons that schedules clerks did not have direct contact with the garages was because of the sensitive relations with the Trade Unions and working practices. The kind of duty that a crew was prepared to work varied from garage to garage although most garages would accept a duty of eight hours in length plus a few minutes. However Chelmsford Garage was quite inflexible. The duties there had a length of seven hours and fifty minutes with only one or two going up to eight hours. There was also a local agreement that duties did not include more than three hours of town services.

Against this background of strong Trade Union input into the way that duties were compiled, it is all the more amazing that in my time at Eastern National one man operation (and it was one man!) and spread-over duties (split shifts) were introduced. These achievements by "the powers that be" led by the General Manager, Mr. Richards, should be recognised for the feats of industrial diplomacy that they must have required.

If my memory serves me right, the first one man operators were at Southend Garage and involved the Wallasea Bay group of routes. They were worked by Bristol LS vehicles which had Setright ticket machines placed rather awkwardly on a bracket to the left and slightly behind the driver; so that he had to turn half-left each time he had to issue tickets. The position of the machine was later moved to a more sensible place on the driver's cab-door.

After the initial introduction of OMO buses, nearly every garage soon had one or two buses at least. Many were the newly introduced Bristol SC4LKs which seated 35 passengers. These were very neat vehicles but I doubt if they would have won any prizes for acceleration and speed. Having said that, I notice that some Alexander-Dennis Darts a few years ago had engines not much bigger than SCs: no doubt they are turbo-charged!

One other matter of interest is that the City Coach take-over included the Brentwood Local services. These included Brentwood to Shotgate (253), to Ongar, Warley and Dunton Wayletts (all 260) as well as a Brentwood Town Service (252). However, with the assimilation of City operations into Eastern National operations, Brentwood Garage gained some work on the 30 (Chelmsford to London Bow) and the 40 (Chelmsford to Tilbury Ferry via Brentwood). This brought some interesting vehicles into the Chelmsford area.

One Saturday afternoon a friend from the Traffic Office and I went to Brentwood to have a ride on the new prototype Routemaster coach which had an ECW body and Leyland engine (then numbered CRL4, later RMC4). I imagine that this was 1958. We waited patiently at the 721 Green Line stop until the Routemaster arrived. We decided that time only permitted a ride to Stratford. Thus we alighted at Stratford Broadway and found the EN Service 30 stop for a ride back to Chelmsford. Much to our delight, the vehicle which appeared was an ex-City Daimler CVD6 with Roberts low-bridge body of Brentwood Garage (from the NVX 171–176 batch). When we left Stratford the bus was well filled and we had a smooth journey to Chelmsford.

Chelmsford Garage being the one nearest to Central Works had an allocation of float vehicles to cover for buses that had run into Chelmsford for repair and overhaul. Until they were needed (typically at weekends), Chelmsford used them on its own routes. Thus one evening I saw a Chelmsford driver on the Service30/40 Stand at Chelmsford Bus Station in the cab of a Brentwood Lodekka (LD6B). He was holding up six fingers to a colleague and pointing to the bonnet to indicate that the bus had a six-cylinder engine: such was the novelty!

Another interesting and serious incident happened on the way home to Hadleigh on the 5.35pm 11A Service. We were travelling on the usual Southend Bristol KSW (of the UEV/UVX batch) and on the main road between Howe Green and Rettendon, the driver tried to overtake the vehicle in front. He must have misjudged the proximity of the off-side kerb and touched it. The bus, in a strange, slow almost graceful movement, turned onto its side and came to rest on the off-side verge. It is the only time that I have had to use the upstairs rear emergency exit door on a double-decker and I do not want to have to do so again! No one was seriously hurt. On the upper-deck we were fairly tightly packed together on the four person bench seats so that we could not move a lot anyway! This must have been in 1957 when fuel supplies were short because of the Suez Crisis. I seem to remember that Mr. Richards, the General Manager, was travelling on this bus to his home in Southend. He was thus saving fuel by not using his company car.

In 1958 my father decided to go into semi-retirement and we moved to Holland-on-Sea, near Clacton. At the time British Railways was promoting the Clacton Branch as a good place from which to commute to London. The fares were very reasonable and the service was being speeded up with the introduction of "Britannia" Pacific locomotives. My father generously agreed to pay for my season ticket from Clacton to Chelmsford in order to facilitate the move. Coincidentally my interest in railways had been growing because from the office at New Writtle Street, we had a good view of the London to Norwich main line and I became fascinated by the procession of Britannias, B1s, B12s and B17s that we were able to see.

I had always had an interest in railways but there is no railway station at Hadleigh and my interest was only cultivated by the occasional trips from Leigh to London and the sight of trains on the LTS line as they crossed the marshes at Hadleigh and when we played as children at Hadleigh Castle. Sometimes we crossed the railway line at an uncontrolled level-crossing in order to walk to the sea-wall between Benfleet and Leigh-on-Sea. On other occasions we walked across "The Saddle-Bank" from Hadleigh Castle to Leigh Station and went on to enjoy a plate of cockles at the cockle sheds. There we could see the LTS trains close at hand.

After a year or so of commuting from Clacton to Chelmsford, it became clear that it was not fair to expect my father to continue to pay for my travel to work and I decided to look for other employment in the transport industry. Eventually I answered an advertisement from British Railways for Traffic apprentices. I applied and was interviewed by Mr. Few, who was the Traffic Manager of the Great Eastern Line, and Mr. Rowett, the Head of Central Timing and Diagramming (C T and D). It was a good interview and, although I was not offered an apprenticeship, I was offered a post in C T and D. I gave Eastern National my resignation and duly left at the end of August 1959. However, before I left, I endured an uncomfortable interview with Mr. Bryan, the Traffic Manager, who clearly thought that I was being less than loyal as far as Eastern National was concerned. He pointed out that it was I who had approached them for a job and they could have reasonably expected more from me. Perhaps he had a point, but the fact was that I could no longer afford to work for them and my prospects there did not seem very bright both financially and career-wise.

Finally, I would like to record that I am grateful for my time at Eastern National. I learnt a lot, made some good friends and enjoyed my work very much indeed. I am also grateful to two Eastern National colleagues the late Bob Beaumont and Ray Boreham, for jogging my memory and helping with some of the historical facts.

RTC

1967–1973 at Head Office

My first ever visit to Head Office & Central Works took place on a Saturday morning in April 1967 when I attended an interview with Mr Jack Healey the Assistant Traffic Manager. It seems I made a good impression as a few days later a letter arrived offering me a job after I finished school in the July. I must have been really keen, as I commenced work on Monday 24th July 1967, having left school the previous Friday. My starting wage was £5 7s 2d (£5.36p) a week, although after six months I received the Traffic Manager's discretionary rise of 10s (50p) a week.

So what do I remember of my first day? Having spent the previous five years travelling to school in Colchester, I was now heading towards Chelmsford. At first it was difficult to make the journey from my Great Totham home by bus without leaving really early, so on his way to work at Ulting my Dad took me via Heybridge where I got a lift with long time friend Terry Smith who worked in the schedules department. I was also put in the schedules department under the wing of Ralph Stevens, who looked after timetable production. He took me on a quick introductory tour of the other Traffic related departments on the first floor and then downstairs to wages where I was allocated clock number T19. I was then issued with a privilege ticket which entitled me to free travel to/from work and staff copies of the ENOC and Southend Area timetable books, both of which I still have today. Then into Chelmsford to get me a National Insurance number. There were no vending machines back then and each morning and afternoon we went across to the office staff canteen inside Central Works. So that only half of those in each department were absent at any one time, we had two sittings.. Everyone was very friendly and there was lots of what I soon realised as a 16 year old was regarded as normal office banter and practical joking.

After a few weeks making up timetable masters using a sharp knife and lots of cow gum, it was decided that I should spend time in other departments and I moved to the extended tours department, which was also home to the ET chartroom. Initially I was put to work collating replies to a questionnaire that had been completed by those travelling on the 1967 tours programme. Later I was shown the many aspects of the work involved in running the department. When the time came, the Tours Superintendent decided that he didn't want me to move on, so that is where I stayed. Little did I know that this decision would ultimately lead to me leaving ENOC behind, or was it that ENOC left me behind?

When Terry moved, my journey to work changed. Now Dad took me to Nounsley to get a bus there and I recall that Jim Brown from Central Works who lived in that village used to catch the same bus. This journey was worked by KN and always an ex Moore's Guy Arab. Coming home I had a choice of routes back to Great Totham, 53/153 to Witham then 335/7 or 31 via Danbury/96 via Hatfield Peverel both to Maldon then 105. In the mornings, following timetable changes, it was possible to catch a service 337 from outside my house to Witham and then a 53 from Witham to Chelmsford. The 337 journey was worked by a great group of KN OMO drivers who would wait for me and if I wasn't working my Mum had to go out and tell them.

Subsequently the decision was made to move the extended tours department to Fairfax Drive in Westcliff-on-Sea (aka Prittlewell) and my time at Head Office came to an end. Along with the other staff that transferred I now found myself working for Tillings Travel (NBC) Limited. However, this wasn't quite the end for at first Tillings didn't have a large format photocopier so after collating the information I returned each week to Head Office to make numerous copies of the tour departure/ return arrangements on their Xerox 720 machine. The 720 referred to the number of copies it should have been able make in an hour, but it used to get so hot that fires and breakdowns were a regular occurrence.

SP

1971–1974 at Head Office

I grew up in Witham and attended secondary school in Colchester so had nearly seven years of travel by service 53 to and from school. My morning journey was on a Chelmsford (CF) depot FLF working but on reaching Kelvedon (KN) there was a crew change and a KN crew took over. The CF crew then collected a Guy from KN depot and worked this back to Chelmsford.

My return journey from school was always on a KN Guy until my last year in sixth form when the 53 was converted to OMO and if I dropped back a departure from Colchester I had the delight of an OMO RE driven at speed by the KN OMO drivers. My morning journey by this time had reverted to a KN Guy working even though the main 53 service was now OMO.

I left school during the summer of 1971 and gained employment with Eastern National at Head Office, Chelmsford as a schedules clerk. My journey to work now took me in the opposite direction from Witham and I travelled on KN OMO REs in both directions which were hugely enjoyable.

The schedules office at that time was headed up by Charlie English as Schedules Officer. I, as a trainee, was put under the wing of Terry Smith who looked after Southend (SD), Hadleigh (HH), Canvey (CY) and Wood Green (WG) depots, plus the 151/251 schedules for Basildon (BN) and Brentwood (BD) too. Other members of the schedules team who I can recall were Eric Carter who looked after BN, Paul Hook for BD, Ray Boreham for Braintree (BE) and Halstead (HD) plus a number more of us; it was a large team in those days. John Dowsett who looked after timetable publicity also shared a desk in the same office.

My early tasks were the mundane jobs of using the ammonia machine to copy bus and crew graphs and then using the plastic sleeve sealing machine to prepare duty cards. I was eager to learn more about scheduling but this didn't come my way until I had completed more mundane tasks such as mileage and urban bonus calculations on the duty cards. However I was soon assisting Terry with the schedules for SD, HH and CY. Later on I moved on to the 151/251 schedules which were very complicated. There were 25 buses on the schedule from SD, CY, BN, BD & WG depots which finished up at different depots to where they had started from – but of course it had to balance up. That was the relatively easy part – then came the crew schedules which were much more difficult to construct. The buses turned at WG in 17 minutes, but the crews stepped back for a break and BD and BN crews took over and came off part way along the route. It was common to have passenger movements to balance the crew schedules but of course this was unproductive and had to be minimised.

The other main attraction of SD, HH and CY schedules was the Southend Coordination Agreement with Southend Corporation Transport. There was a strict mileage balance, 63% ENOC and 37% SCT, and the share of timetables had to be carefully worked out. I attended these meetings with Terry and Derek Giles from SCT on many occasions.

My time came to an end in the schedules office in 1974 as I was transferred to CF depot as a Traffic Assistant. This was a totally different experience at the sharp end of bus operation. Staff shortages were rife at this time and lost mileage was not uncommon. It was all about recruitment and retention.

My Traffic Manager at that time was Bob Hanley and he put my name forward for the NBC Senior Management Training Scheme which I was successful in being selected. I sadly left Eastern National in December 1974 for a new start with Midland Red in Birmingham.

KS

North Western Road Car to the rescue!

I was a traffic clerk at Head Office working in the Coaching Department in the 1960's This department dealt with the developing extended tour programme of the Company which in 1964 offered more than twenty coach holidays throughout England, Scotland and Wales. It was exciting times with weekly departures during the summer from most of the network and from London where control of the Tillings Travel operation had taken place in 1962. I got involved with most of the work from taking bookings from Company offices' and agents to planning the routes of the tours, booking hotels for lunch, dinner, bed and breakfast.

I did not deal with the vehicle and drivers allocated for the tours. The majority of the drivers were an elite group, most of them handpicked from a pool of ex Westcliff-on-Sea Motor Services from Southend depot. What therefore happened on a late Friday afternoon was a surprise and a challenge! All in the department had left for the day and likewise I was about to as well when the phone rang and the driver of the coach returning from Scotland said he had broken down in the Derbyshire Peak District. I ascertained where he was and sought out the Tilling and B.E.T. office/depot books, which were the bus bibles of the day for all major operators. The nearest depot to the location of the breakdown was Buxton under the control of North Western Road Car. The driver said he could limp to Buxton where the overnight stay for the tour was and would see if a repair could be carried out. Job done, I thought and on returning to the office on Monday, I was told that North Western had decided to loan the Company one of their coaches complete with driver to enable the tour to finish on time in London and Essex. The Eastern National driver was to return with the repaired coach the next day. No doubt North Western supplied a Leyland or perhaps an A.E.C. coach, although the depot engineers at Buxton had experience of Bristol vehicles, as they still operated Bristol single deck L types during 1964.

This event sparked another series of robust discussions between the Coaching Superintendent and the Chief Engineer. For some time the

In Scotland in the summer of 1964. ENOC coach No.559, OO 9545, Bristol MW6G takes a rest for lunch at Moffat, Dumfries and Galloway on a 12-day tour. This is not the coach that the North Western Road Car Company rescued at Buxton!

coach fleet was feeling its age and a mix of Bristol LS and MW types were used on extended tours and the view was that newer coaches with six cylinder engines were required to undertake the extended tour programme which were beginning to include fast running on the newly constructed motorways of the M1 and the M6. Almost weekly, there were discussions with the Chief Engineer to improve the coach fleet including the removal of the Company's policy of governing engines to a maximum speed to save on fuel. It was an experience I found out for myself when we used a new Bristol RE for a private hire using the M1, but found ourselves being overtaken on numerous occasions by the faster coaches of North Western, Ribble and Midland Red. I think we managed 50 m.p.h. flat out!

The next few years would see a number of coach swaps between the Eastern National and Tilling fleets and gradually the age profile of the coach fleet improved, particularly as Tillings had newer Bristol MW's and RE's from 1964. I left the Company in 1966 with this memory, but whilst my parents went on a few coaching holidays, I never had the chance to actually sample one.

AG

Memories – On the buses with operating staff

Conducting and Driving at Wood Green

I left school at Christmas 1954 and started work the day after Boxing Day, in those days January 1st was not a public holiday. I started at a company that manufactured suitcases called S. Noton Ltd, their factory was at the Standard, Walthamstow, which was the old AEC works where years earlier the first buses for London General had been built. I was taken on as an apprentice to learn factory maintenance at two pounds ten shillings per week (£2.50). Down in the huge cellar which had not been used for very many years we did eventually find half a dozen old General engines covered in thick rust. Being a young lad I did not understand the history of our find; they were still there in 1957 when I left the company.

My mates were earning up to twelve pounds a week and I was still on four pounds a week in 1957 and I wanted a car and girlfriends but could not afford them! However early in 1957 I saw an advert for conductors with Eastern National (EN) at Wood Green (WG) depot. I wrote in and got an interview there with Tom Newbold, the Garage Manager, which I attended in his office above the EN travel shop. It was a good interview and I felt very easy with Mr Newbold; he took me down into the garage and introduced me to some of the office staff and a few members of the WG road staff and then into the shed for a look at some of the buses. Mr Newbold gave me a start on a Monday morning a week later, giving me time to hand in my week's notice. WG was of course the former City Coach Company and latterly Westcliff Motor Services depot in north London which operated the so-called "main road" service, Wood Green to Southend via Romford, Brentwood, Billericay, Wickford and Rayleigh. The service had been allocated number 251 in 1953 in the scheme that EN instituted to accommodate the ex Westcliff and City routes and was the only route operated by WG at this time.

I duly started the following Monday with Johnny Jackson, the trainer for conductors, on duty 11 [all our duties were l followed by the duty number], which was the first one out at 0525 on the Monday morning. Mr Amott the duty inspector [jumper] gave me a pass and John introduced me to his driver, then told me to sit in the lower saloon. I was instructed to take notice of as much detail as I could and to listen to him call out where we were, as it was a two week training period and by next Monday he would expect me to be doing the job under his guidance.

What he did not tell me that on a Monday the public bought their weekly tickets, either 5-day or 6-day, so it was a busy trip. The 251 road was a two and a half hour run and I was not used to being up at that hour so I fell asleep! John woke me up just out of Wickford and was not too upset with me. We got into Tylers Avenue depot in Southend at eight and went into the café. We did not have to operate a Rayleigh or Wickford short, so we were back in WG by twelve. When we got back I was given my uniform and told that I was with John all week; the following week I would be on late turn, again with John. The training went well and John gave me all sorts of tips to make the job flow in an easy fashion. I think that we started our late turn on Sunday afternoon. On the Monday we had a Wickford short which we did with one of Southend depot's LS or older L5G single deckers which we called conker boxes. The reason for a single decker was that the old railway bridge at Shotgate was too low for double deckers.

At WG we had a spare crew sign on at 5.15am called early show up (ESU) and a late crew sign on at about 1200 which was late show up (LSU). If you did not go out on either duties covering for sickness, on most of the times that I did the duty, I helped out in the transport office preparing the Setright ticket machines for the following day and counting the money coming in. On a Friday we would go down to the bank in Wood Green High Road by car with one of the garage inspectors to collect the shed's wages.

Once I had gone through my training with flying colours I was put with an elderly ex-City driver by the name of Bill Eves, I think that he was in his late sixties and not in the best of health; his breathing was not too good, he always had the driver's blind down at the back of the cab and his wife always came with him and sat in the seat behind the cab. When I started with him, he told me just to look after the bell and he would take care of the rest. He knew every time of the services, such as whether the 11 duty should be in front of or behind us. On one week we were doing the last bus home, the 9.25pm out of Southend. We should have had a Southend crew three minutes in front of us [we called them swingers] working up to Brentwood to clear the short runners [rabbits], leaving us with the through passengers. The jumper at Tylers Avenue would push this particular crew out on time and we would go on ours, by the time we had got to the Southend Road we were past him and for the first three nights we never saw them again. On the fourth night, I think that Bill might have said something to the jumper, Bill told me to just get going on the bell, I did and we went up to Kent Elms Corner at Eastwood like a rocket, so that by the time we got to Rayleigh High Street we were well early. Bill flashed the saloon lights and called me round to him and told me that he was going to pull into the speedway car park just beyond Rayleigh Station and sit quietly there for a short while. He did so and out went all the lights. I told the rabbits what it was all about, then we watched our swinger go past quite fast looking for us! Bill pulled out and we pushed him along, staying a couple of stops behind him all the way up to Brentwood – he was busy and not very happy!

Bill died a few months later and Tom Newbold let us take one of the Leylands to his funeral with a crowd of us and his wife. There was a clippie by the name of Maureen working with Harry Winsor, another ex-City driver, I did ask her out but she would not have any of it. She decided to leave the job, so I got a transfer to work behind Harry as his regular conductor. He was another driver that knew the job well, but I used to lose him when he did some private hire and station transfers with the Bristol MWs. We had a driver by the name of Tom Day who would do all the overtime going – in fact we called him "double day" – the overtime was two Southend rounders which amounted to about a fifteen hour day for a driver. The Rayleigh and Wickford shorts normally on the duties were instead covered by Southend staff, to keep within the driving hours. I also did a lot of doubles but as a conductor I had to do the shorts as well, but the money was good and it enabled me to buy a 1951 Austin A40 for £250 and pass my driving test in late 1957.

Road staff at WG were represented by the Transport and General Workers Union and John Jackson's brother Bill, a driver at WG, was the union rep. He quite soon got made up to an inspector; now we had two jumpers, Bill and Mr Amott. They were quite fair if they found something amiss, most of the time they would just quietly advise you and that was that. A prank that we used to play on the punters was if you had a Leyland such as BD 1139 (FJN 205) – once we had left Wickford and climbed up Runwell Chase [at that time there was a mental hospital at Runwell], we did a right turn onto Hawk Hill to run down into Battlesbridge. Just after the turn there was a railway bridge under the Southminster branch line and from our position on the road you could see over the top of it. The seats on the upper deck of the Leyland's were the standard lowbridge pattern of four across to the nearside – we would stand at the top of the stairs and call out "mind your heads please" and it was amazing how many people did duck their heads as we went down the bank and safely under the bridge!

Wood Green in the summer months did a few extras on nice sunny days, the idea was to work the bus down as normal mixing in with the service buses and you could have a domino load [a full capacity load of punters] by the time we had reached Walthamstow The Bell public house, then it was three bells until someone alighted and we would arrive slightly early in Tylers Avenue, but no notice was taken of that. We would drop our punters off and run up to Southend shed dead and park the bus up, then make our own way back to WG, most times we would get a lift up the Southend Road to the Waterworks Corner in Woodford and then catch the next service back to WG. Our name for this bit of overtime was a slash and we would get a couple of hours for nothing.

We had one duty that signed on at 6.10am and ran down dead [private] to the King's Head at Great Burstead and we worked back to WG as a swinger to a Southend crew, normally working the stops one for one and although it was busy job it made an easy job. One bus we had was WG 1489 with the Cave-Brown-Cave heating system which was a good motor but in my time as her conductor it used to get very hot up on the top deck as the front windows were fixed non openers. At this time 236 LNO, BD1541, appeared – a seventy seater which we called Big Bertha. She was a superb bus to conduct as she had a good turn of speed (6 cylinder engine and 5-speed overdrive gearbox) and was a good motor to have on late turns out of WG when you caught all the runners finishing work from Gesteners, Lebus and Ever Ready's factories going out through Tottenham and Walthamstow. At the time the minimum fare was six pence (2½p) as against London Transport's three pence, so on a late turn back into WG we would try to get behind a 625 trolleybus somewhere through Walthamstow and scratch him back to WG. That way we could do our waybill and takings en route, so that when we got outside WG all we had to do was run our box and Setright into the office, unlock our cubby hole, put the box in and drop our takings and waybill into the night safe, while our driver took the bus round the back and parked it on the fuel pump for the night staff – then we were gone.

One sad event happened to a driver by the name of Harry Brocklebank, known to us as Brock, he was a very smart guy – collar and tie, white shirt and he wore gloves to drive. One morning at Kent Elms Corner in Eastwood he knocked a child down with an LD Lodekka in the pouring rain, the child finished up underneath the bus. Brock got underneath the bus on the wet road and gave comfort and held the child while the fire brigade jacked up the bus and got the child out and as luck would have it the child only suffered from shock.

After a couple of years conducting, as described last month, by now it was going into 1960 and I had a car driving licence and I wanted to "go on the front" ie get a bus driver's licence. I asked the Garage Manager, Tom Newbold, and it turned out that I was one of three conductors with the same idea. Tom arranged for us all to go out with Tommy Flavell, another ex City man, and he would teach us to drive a bus.

We started with the Leyland deckers as they had a synchromesh box and were therefore a bit easier to drive than Bristols. Tommy took us all around Wood Green and Tottenham [there was no driving school at WG] then we slowly went onto Bristol LDs to learn the art of a smooth change with a crash box. The LDs had a five speed box where 5th is an overdrive ratio, selected out of 4th rather than from the main gearbox gate. Therefore it was essential to make sure you did not stop in 5th because it is near impossible to get 4th out of fifth! Six months later we had our test around the west end of London with a Leyland PD2, BD 1139 (FJN 205) and we all got through. Now I was on the front and by this time the Bristol FLFs had started to arrive – the 251 had all the TVXs from 1571 to 1590 (80–99 TVX, later renumbered 2700–19).

When the first FLF arrived at WG in 1960 it was in the middle of the week and it was parked up by the canteen stairs on the left hand side just below the main garage doors, this is viewed from the office. As we had never seen a FLF before and being totally different from the rear platform style, all the shed staff were told to have a good look round her. The bus was WG 1571, 80 TVX, and she went to work on the following Saturday. Beyond this look round, there was no type training, we just went out and learnt by our own mistakes. We did find that due to the camber on the road at times the doors on the FLFs would not close, or we forgot to close them, so we would get a frantic knocking on the small cab window.

One morning at about 1100 in the summer by this time we had a good few FLFs and we were working back to WG with one. I got into Rayleigh and pulled into the lay-by for the bus stop; I just sat and watched the traffic in my mirrors, waiting for the bell. The bell went and I eased out of the lay-by and into the traffic to turn left down Crown Hill to Rayleigh station. As I straightened up down the hill I got a mass of bells so I pulled into the nearside, opened the doors, got out and went round and onto the bus, when I got on there was a lot of laughter on the lower saloon. My conductor was at the back of the bus so I made my way to him, a woman was stood by the rear emergency door, covered in white as were the punters sitting on either side of the door. By all accounts as I had eased away and turned left down the hill, the woman who had got on at the stop was holding a large cream cake in front of her had got into a slow trot and ran into the back of the bus with this cream cake in front of her. The cake promptly exploded and covered all around her and herself in thick cream! The punters were in fits of laughter as I was! She was laughing and said it was just one of those things and in a way it was her own fault as she should have sat down at the front of the bus. I went on down to the station and phoned Brentwood from a public phone box. They gave us a replacement bus in Brentwood High Street which was an LD. There were comments made about the state of the rear of the bus, so my conductor said when we spoke back in WG. We never heard any more about it and the punters were laughing for a long time about it.

I did earn good money with my double days and on a Saturday night if the office could not get a WG crew to cover a late run in, they would get a Brentwood crew to do it and as I had not long passed my test, they would give me three hours to run the crew back to Brentwood in my car, which gave me a bit more experience in driving. I remember the names of some of the staff – Tom Newbold was garage manager, Mr Amott and Bill Jackson traffic inspectors, Tom Flavell driving instructor/driver, Harry Winsor driver/private hire driver, Johnny Coulton, Tom Day, Harry Brocklebank, Bill Eves and Tom Worrell all drivers, Maureen Askem clippie, John Jackson conductor/trainer, John Clevleys conductor [who every Friday afternoon went up to the canteen and managed to lose his wages playing cards, as you might gather he was hopeless at cards], Pat clippie [did not like late turns] and Charles Jukes garage foreman; he used to come up that garage in a bus like there was no tomorrow! Jim Blazeby did the refuelling and washing of the buses and always wore a black beret. The wash was just inside the exit door on the right and lifted up and down over the bus from the roof of the shed.

The buses that I remember were the 1500s (Bristol Lodekkas, in both LD & FLF versions), the Leyland PD2s, the LSs which we would get now and again from WG and on the shorts from Southend, the L5Gs or as we called them "conker boxes" on the Southend shorts, and the old ex City Coach Company Daimler double deckers. The latter had pre-selector gearboxes which have a change speed pedal in place of a conventional clutch. As many drivers have found to their cost, if you did not move your feet quickly enough, they would give you a kick from the sprung loaded pedal. Woe betide the driver who forgot and tried to ride the pedal like a clutch! (Later when on LT, I discovered that their pre-selectors were air operated and didn't kick back).

Every year WG would send two or three open top deckers ex Southend to Epsom for the Derby and although I never got to go, by all accounts it was a fine day out sitting on the top deck watching the racing and eating the freshly prepared food. I think that my favourite bus was 236 LNO [BD 1541], the 30' long LDL model and I am glad that she is still with us in Canvey Museum and I do thank Craig Mara and his father for doing a good job in looking after her. I do think that the Lodekka's were a good tool and well built even with their crash boxes and a lot of what I learnt in those years with EN lasted me for the next fifty years.

To end with, a couple of short stories that took place in my time on EN. A Brentwood fitter was out on test with a Bristol K, having done some work on it, and he took it down the bank through Harold Wood but he knocked it out of gear and eventually the prop shaft came up through the floor and did a reasonable amount of damage, it was a good thing that he was running dead! What the outcome of this was, I do not know. We could not catch the RTs on the Greenline service up through Harold Wood – they would pass us like we were standing still, it was not so bad with 6 pot (6 cylinder engined bus) but with a 5 pot it was quite embarrassing. On one early afternoon start out of WG we had so much layover time in Brentwood that I can remember going to the pictures to see Elvis Presley in G.I Blues and then on another day, spending time window shopping up and down the High Street, but times have changed.

It always seemed a long way home on a dark foggy, rainy night in the middle of winter up through Battlesbridge into Wickford and very few passengers about but it was a good job and I did enjoy it. I left the National in about 1962 as I wanted to go long distance HGV driving. I ran for Harry Lebus out of Tottenham and used to do Aberdeen, Inverness and up to Wick and Thurso. That lasted until 1969 when I went up to Manor House [the London Transport Recruitment Centre] as by this time I was married and my late wife June was nagging me about being away too long driving lorries. But that is another story.

MP

EASTERN NATIONAL

Service 10 CHELMSFORD—LONDON (BOW)

REVISED TERMINAL POINT AT LONDON (BOW)

Commencing

SUNDAY, 24th SEPTEMBER, 1950

THIS SERVICE WILL CEASE TO USE THE L.M.R. STATION FORECOURT BUT WILL BE SLIGHTLY EXTENDED AND WILL ARRIVE AT AND DEPART FROM THE JUNCTION OF BOW ROAD AND TOMLIN'S GROVE (THE TURNING IMMEDIATELY BEFORE THE RAILWAY OVER-BRIDGE) AND ONLY A FEW YARDS SHORT OF THE BOW ROAD "UNDERGROUND" STATION.

EN.AD. 5792/30850.   Head Offices : New Writtle Street, Chelmsford.   'Phone 3431 (4 lines).   [Exhibit until 14/10/50.

All change at Bow with this ENOC notice dating from 1950 for display inside buses. Service 10 became Service 30 on 18th September, 1955 before withdrawal on 7th January, 1968. The LMR station at Bow is erroneous as the station was actually under the control of the North London Railway and then subsequently the London Midland and Scottish Railway and closed on 15th May, 1944. There are minor remains of the station and Tomlin's Grove remains extant as a residental street with no buses!

Right: MP may have left Wood Green Depot (WG) earlier in 1962, before this scene was captured in December of the same year. ENOC bus No. 1616, EOO 582 Bristol FLF6G, not allocated to WG, heads towards Wood Green on a snow-bound Forest Road in Walthamstow.

Finchingfield in 1958. Perhaps the most illustrated village in journals and calendars of Essex, with ENOC bus No. 1370 TNO 681, Bristol KSW5G climbing away from the bridge and duck pond en-route for Braintree on Service 321. PO on page 160 refers to Service 21. This service had originated from Ben Adams and T. Sullens and Son of Finchingfield and then Horn Coaches of Braintree before they sold the business to ENOC on 24th August, 1935. It was renumbered from 21 to 321 on 11th September,1955

Another ENOC, Bristol KSW5G, bus No.2308, SHK512, looking in fine condition as it leaves Bishop's Stortford Interchange en-route for Saffron Walden on Service 301 on 29th September, 1967. The bus was over 16 years old and shows its new number which it acquired when the whole fleet was renumbered in August 1964. The bus was withdrawn by 1969. The sign of the Crown and Rose Public House can be seen and the pub dates from the mid-nineteenth century.

The interloper! ENOC bus No.2514, 351 LPU, Bristol LD5G allocated to Chelmsford depot waits with the conductor inside Bishop's Stortford depot before a short Thursdays only working to Takeley on Service 70. "Takley" is shown on the destination blind which is obviously mis-spelt! The date of this shot is unknown, but probably in the early 1970's when ENOC was part of the National Bus Company. The garage building survives today as a tyre depot.

Conducting and Driving at Clacton-on-Sea

My year at the Bernard Gilpin Society at Durham came to an end in June 1965 and the next part of my theological education at St. Aidan's College Birkenhead was due to begin in September. In the meantime it was essential that I should get some seasonal work in order to remain financially solvent. The logical thing was to try to do something that was both seasonal and enjoyable. I therefore applied to the Clacton Garage of Eastern National as a seasonal conductor.

My application was successful and on the first Monday of my vacation I joined the conductors' training course at Clacton Bus Station. The course lasted one week and began with an arithmetic test, which I passed. We then went on to learn how to use the Setright Speed ticket machine and how to fill in the way-bill. We were also taught how to read time-tables and fare-tables. Of course this was not difficult for me having worked as a schedules clerk. I had also had some experience of fare-tables as the whole of the traffic office at Chelmsford had done overtime preparing new fare-tables each time there was a fare-revision (increase!). In those days they had to be submitted to the Traffic Commissioner for approval.

We were told that way-bills should be filled in at every fare-stage which seems amazing today and was very optimistic then. We were also taught how to make out transfer way-bills and transfer tickets. These were used if it was necessary to transfer passengers from one bus to another. This would happen as the result of an accident or when a duplicate journey was cut short when there were not enough passengers to justify two buses. They would also be used when another crew were due to take over a bus en-route: such as on services 19, 19A and 53. Fortunately, I never had to issue a transfer way-bill or transfer tickets. I cannot remember issuing them on the Clacton Town services where the changeover was at the bus station. Perhaps I should have done! I imagine such practices became redundant on buses years ago! I seem to remember that a short time was allocated to route learning.

After a week of training, we were sent out on to the road. However, it was not as brutal as it may sound, as the first week was spent with a senior conductor who acted as a tutor. I was placed with Reg Turner whose regular driver was Reg Old. They were a bus crew of great experience and I could not have hoped for a better introduction to the practical work of being a bus conductor. Reg Turner was a dry "old stick" with an understated sense of humour. Reg Old had a certain authority but was also a very pleasant and supportive driver. They were a great team. I was fortunate enough to work some overtime with Reg Old later on in the summer.

Our first journey was a works service to a factory at Beaumont near Great Oakley and our bus was a Bristol K5G of the ONO batch with, of course, an ECW low-bridge body. After dropping off our passengers at Beaumont, we ran "dead" (light) to Great Oakley to work a peak hour journey to Clacton on service 106. This was a busy journey and as it was Monday morning, it involved the issue of some weekly tickets [these were card tickets issued by inserting them into a slot on the front of the ticket machine, then running off the appropriate value ticket, which printed onto the card rather than the ticket roll].

Reg followed me around the bus to make sure that I was issuing the tickets correctly and giving the right change. After all it was his shift and he would have been responsible for any shortage of money when it came to paying in. The rest of the week was spent on the usual round of shifts on regular rota and we worked on routes to Walton and Colchester as well as some more local services.

It was an enjoyable week and, by the end of it, I must have passed the test as Reg let me run the bus more or less by myself. There were other advantages of spending one's first five days with a regular crew. They introduced me to the secrets of Clacton Garage in Castle Road, the Canteen at the bus station and the process of paying-in.

On the Saturday of this week I was out on the road by myself, or rather with my regular driver, Harry Lau, who was a friend whom I had met through the local church. He was a very fast driver and we had asked to be put together as a crew. On occasions, when working on Service 111, Harry would stop off at Coppins Green, buy some fish and chips, wedge them next to the engine in the cab to keep them warm and eat them in the rest room at the bus station. After about one month, Harry decided that it was time for him to move on and I was put with another driver. I cannot remember his name but we got on well together and worked as a crew for the next two months. However, on overtime it was not unusual to have to work with a different driver.

At this point I should explain that in those days there were three rotas at Clacton Garage during the summer season. There was a One Man Operator (OMO) rota, the Regular crew rota and the Seasonal rota. The OMO men mainly operated the Point Clear (101A), St. Osyth Beach (101B) and Burrsville Circular services, although in the winter months they worked further afield. The regular crews covered mainly the longer distance services and the Seasonal crews the town services. However, there was a certain amount of overlapping and seasonal crews were asked to do overtime on all services. Indeed on the evening of my first Saturday on the road, I worked a service to Walton on an FLF.

On the Seasonal Rota nearly every service we worked ended up at Jaywick Sands: indeed, on some duties we were there every hour! This was not as bad as it sounds as there was a cafe at the terminus that was well-tuned to ministering to the needs of thirsty bus crews on a five minute (or less) turn-round. The main services that we covered were the 110 (Holland to Jaywick via the Main Road and Clacton Hospital), 111 (Holland to Wargrave Road), 112 (Holland to Jaywick via the sea front) and 121 (Highfield Park Caravan Camp to Jaywick). All of these services operated via Clacton Bus Station and took one hour for a round trip. The tightest timings were on the 110 which had only a two minute turn round at each end and was a busy route. This pattern of services provided six buses each hour between Clacton and Jaywick although the 110 did not go via Pier Avenue. The Pier stop was the busiest for picking up passengers for Butlin's Holiday Camp.

The 112 Sea Front service was operated by open-toppers. These were Leyland PD1s which had been converted from covered top vehicles by Eastern National. One of them was an ex-City example with a Beadle body while the other one was an ex-Hicks vehicle with Leyland body. Both had started their lives as low-bridge buses. The conversion work was a fine testimony to the expertise of the Eastern National engineering department. They were 59 seaters. When the weather was wet or very cold, the open-toppers were replaced by normal closed-top buses if possible.

My eldest brother had, by this time, transferred from Hadleigh Garage to Clacton and was an OMO driver. However at times the OMO drivers worked overtime on double-deckers. He once commented that "the Leylands" were too fast for the sea front. What was needed was something that would just "jog along"! I think that he was right.

As already mentioned, seasonal crews were sometimes asked to work overtime, usually half of a shift, on the regular rota. I cannot remember working any further afield than Walton-on-Naze as a conductor, but most overtime seemed to be on town services and the Point Clear (101A) and St. Osyth Beach (101B) roads. Both of these services were operated by single-deckers, Bristol LSs and MWs.

Two incidents come to mind. First, on the last service to St. Osyth Beach one night, we had over 60 passengers on a 45 seater LS simply because we could not leave them behind! The regulation number of standing passengers at that time was eight. I believe it was five on London Transport.

Second, one evening, on a late Point Clear service, we were "jumped" on the outskirts of Clacton, on a very dark St. Osyth Main Road, by two "flying squad" inspectors from outside of the area. There was, presumably, a third one in a car somewhere as there were not many other buses around at that time of night. Whether it was a targeted inspection on me or not, I do not know! Any way they found nothing wrong and went on their way. Perhaps the object of their inspection was the crew who should have been working the shift, bearing in mind that we were on overtime.

We were warned about a number of practices for which there was no excuse. One was the issuing of "two-star tickets", that is tickets with no value on them but just two stars. If these were found on a bus that you had been working on, you would be looked at very closely. Another was a warning about running early. The explanation was simple. There are a hundred reasons for late running, but none for running early!

Turning to the fleet in the Clacton area at that time, the vehicles on the town services were Bristol K's and KSW'S. The OMO vehicles were Bristol LSs and MWs. If my memory serves me right, Bristol FLFs had been introduced and were used mainly on the Walton services along with Bristol LD Lodekkas. The Walton road always had the best buses.

Although there were some Bristol Lodekkas at Clacton, all the regular vehicles on the Town Services, apart from the open-toppers, were of the low bridge type. The upstairs was not easy for passengers and the person at the gangway end of the four passenger seat often had to hold on tight! This was not the case for passengers on the back seat which was tucked away from the gangway over the platform. Low bridge vehicles had one advantage for conductors. The view of the platform in the mirror looking back down the gangway at the platform was excellent, better than on a high-bridge bus. It was therefore possible to "ring off" the bus (give the driver the starting signal) from the front of the bus upstairs. However, I am sure that such practices were not encouraged and in the event of a platform accident, the conductor would have been to blame. Having said that, I am sure that few conductors did not "yield to this temptation" when under pressure.

Another practice that was possible with half-cab vehicles was to "ring off" by giving a couple of sharp taps with a half-a-crown (12.5p) coin or a two shilling (10p) piece on the driver's bulk-head window. This, again, was not a safe practice but a very tempting one. With the advent of the front entrance (FLF) Lodekkas, the driver could see the platform and often started when he could see that it was safe to do so. However, it was often advisable to give a tap on the small window on the drivers cab. Of course, when working on open-toppers the conductor could simply look over the side and see what was going on "down below" and "ring off" by giving the driver a couple of sharp taps on the driver's cab roof with their heel! This was another practice that was not recommended.

For some reason, at this time, the Clacton EN area never had many Bristol KSWs. One of the last (WNO) batch of KSW's was at Walton garage. Six of the WNOs and three of the VNO batch (VNO 858–860), the latter for the 322 service (Braintree to London), had "staggered" seating upstairs. This was a device to try to allocate the correct and fair amount of seating to each passenger on the bench seats upstairs. It did that, but it was very difficult for passengers to get in and out, and it did not help in the collection of fares.

These days (2009) low-bridge buses are often spoken of and written about as though travelling on them was something from the "dark ages". The impression is given that they were little more than cattle trucks. The fact of the matter is that for people who lived in places like Essex they were the norm. Until the advent of the Bristol "Lodekka" and later the Dennis Loline, the AEC Bridgemaster and the Leyland (Albion) Lowlander, low bridge buses were the only way of providing an extra twenty (20) seats over those provided by single-deckers and cope with low bridges of which there are many. Low bridge buses served us well: for many of us, high-bridge buses were unusual and appeared top heavy!

Walton garage worked on the 107 Clacton to Walton route and also had some turns on the 105 from Walton to Colchester. Clacton also worked on the 105 as part of a long round trip: that is Clacton to Walton (107), Walton to Colchester and return (105) and then Walton to Clacton (107). Other garages that worked into Clacton were Dovercourt (104/106) and Colchester (19, 19A and 53).

There was also an out-station that worked into Clacton, or rather, for most of its existence, its vehicle worked into Clacton. This was Ipswich. I do not know the dates when this sequence of events happened, but the general history was something like this. Traditionally an Eastern National double-decker was out-stationed at the Eastern Counties Ipswich Garage with an Eastern National crew. For years this crew worked the Ipswich end of service 123 (Clacton to Ipswich). The 123 was a long, 29 mile route, which made its way from Clacton to Ipswich by way of Thorpe-le-Soken, Tendring, Mistley, Manningtree, Brantham and Holbrook. This was in no way a direct route and the running time was one hour and forty-five minutes. What happened was that the Ipswich crew worked towards Clacton and changed over with a Clacton crew when they met. The second part of the Ipswich crew duty read something like this:-

DD1	6.25pm Car to Stand	
	6.30pm Towards Clacton: change over	123
CN	Car Return to Ipswich	123
	8.30pm Towards Clacton: change over	123
DD1	Return to Ipswich	123
	10.15pm Car to Garage	
	10.20pm Sign Off	
	10.30pm Finish.	

The arrangement was not quite as unorganised as it might seem, as the Ipswich and Clacton crews knew where the change-over point was on each particular journey [looking at the timetables of the period, the 6.30pm and 8.30pm journeys from each end passed in Mistley]. They did not just drive until they met one another! I imagine that these change-overs were occasions when it was necessary to write up a transfer way-bill and leave it on the bus for the next conductor. On rest days and holidays, Eastern Counties provided the crew. The bus, which was out-stationed at Ipswich, was an early post-war Bristol K5G. At some time in the early 1960s, it was decided that the Ipswich crew should work through to Clacton on the evening journeys. This meant, of course, that the Clacton crews would work through to Ipswich. My brother told me that the first time that the Ipswich crew worked through to Clacton, all the crews at Clacton Bus Station turned out to cheer them in! Some years later, the 123 became a joint service with Eastern Counties taking on the responsibility for the Ipswich allocation.

After three interesting and enjoyable months, my time as a conductor at Clacton Garage came to an end. It was time for me to move to Birkenhead for the next part of my training for ordination. However, this period in my life proved to be very interesting both from a theological point of view and an "omnibological" point of view. It also turned out to be the saddest period in my life.

In September 1967 I returned to St. Aidan's College in Birkenhead, to begin my final year of theological training. Among other things, I thought that it would be good to be among friends who knew me and cared for me. And so it turned out. The staff and students at the college helped me through the most difficult period of my life.

I was due to be ordained in 1968 and as I was from Chelmsford Diocese I wrote to the Bishop of Chelmsford. In one way and another it was decided that I should be a curate in the parish of Billericay. However as I would not be ordained until September 1968, it would be necessary for me to find a seasonal job for the summer of 1968. My other home, besides college, was the home of my late wife's mother in Clacton. My own mother had died in 1967. I therefore wrote to Eastern National at Clacton and offered my services as a conductor (having worked there in summer 1965,) but I also mentioned that I had spent some time on the Crosville driving school at Rock Ferry in 1967. As a result I was invited to join the driving school at Clacton during the Easter vacation.

On the first Monday of the vacation I reported to Clacton Bus Station and joined the 'learner-bus'. It was a Bristol KSW5G registered TNO 685 (2331). Like the Crosville Lodekka I had learnt on the previous year, it had a wooden framed, removable bulk-head window behind the driver. The driving instructor was an Inspector. He drove the bus to the sea-front on the Holland-on-Sea side of Clacton and I was invited to climb into the driver's cab. It was more of a climb than the Lodekka because the KSW has a higher driving position, which I grew to appreciate.

The instructor, a rather brusque Inspector who hailed from Yorkshire, explained to me that 2331 had a five-cylinder engine. As a result, it had an 'odd beat' and it would be a little more difficult to obtain a smooth gear-change than with the 6-cylinder Gardner in the Crosville Lodekka I'd driven previously. By taking my time, I managed to perfect good gear changes. The second piece of advice that the Inspector gave me I have always remembered. It was when I was driving along a main road in North Essex which had high hedges, he said: "Don't sit up there taking your time! Look over the top of the hedges and, if there is nothing coming, cut the corners." It was good advice and speeded up the progress of the bus considerably.

There were about half-a-dozen of us in the driving school and we took it in turns to have a drive. When we were not driving most of us lounged around on the bench seats upstairs on this low-bridge bus. The area that we travelled around was roughly bounded by Clacton, Elmstead Market, Manningtree and Harwich. When it was time for one of us to have a driving test we ran into Colchester. However, as often as not, those not involved were dropped off somewhere convenient and made their way home. Some days, we had a coffee break at the cafe at the service station at Little Bentley Corner on the A133. We tucked 2331 away out of sight in the corner of the car-park under some trees. Well, as far as one can tuck a double-decker bus away out of sight!

Of course there was a lot more to the driving course than riding around in a double-decker bus, as picturesque and delightful as the North Essex countryside is. We also had to learn and practice the other skills associated with normal driving, such as reversing and parking. We were encouraged to reverse using only the driving mirrors, although I believe it was allowed for drivers to look through the open platform of a rear entrance bus. Anyway, the trick was to identify the nearside wheel arch in the mirror and focus attention on that. We were also told that the examiner would ask us what kinds of obstacles we should be aware of when driving a double-decker. These are low-bridges, overhanging trees and shop-blinds.

We were also given experience in driving Bristol FLF double-deckers and LS or MW under floor-engined single-deckers. This happened when the regulator at Clacton Bus Station was able to spare the FLF learner bus. Like 2331 it had a wooden-framed removable bulk-head window. Due to the front entrance and staircase this was, of course a lot smaller than that on 2331. I sometimes wonder whether the regulator ever thought that 2331, a KSW, was a fair exchange for an FLF. The FLF experience was so that we could have some experience of driving a thirty-foot long double-decker with a front entrance with electrically operated doors. It was also so that we could learn how to use the five-speed gear-box and, in particular, how to find the fifth gear. The secret was that there is a second 'gate' near to the fourth gear. One held the gear-lever towards one's body, slid it forward to the 'gate', double-declutched and slid the gear-lever into the fifth gear. Like most things, 'it was easy when you knew how'. However it was important to remember to pull the gear-lever towards yourself when going for fifth and to hold it away from your body when changing down to third. Later on, one of the drivers in the school told me that he had forgotten the correct procedure when changing down to third on the rise between Holland Road School and the Roaring Donkey. He got fifth instead and the bus almost ground to a halt!

Having discovered how to find fifth gear, the object was to use it for the purpose for which it was fitted, that is cruising at speeds of 30mph and over. The only place to do this in those days (1968) was the A133 between Weeley and Elmstead Market. This we did. However on one occasion the unfortunate member of the driving school in the cab came to a halt at some temporary traffic lights at Elmstead Market with the FLF in fifth gear. He tried to change it to second gear to re-start the bus but he could not move it. The traffic lights changed but he could not move the bus and we waved the following traffic past us. In the end the instructor got in the cab and managed to pull the gear-lever out of fifth with two hands and a lot of effort. Thus we learnt another lesson: do not stop in fifth gear if at all possible!

Another purpose of the FLF experience was to introduce us to the air-braking system fitted to the FLF vehicles. This braking system is a lot more powerful than the vacuum brakes fitted to the other buses and it was good to have some instruction about how to use them without throwing the passengers around the bus when approaching a stop.

We were told that, in theory at least, the gear-box on LS and MW single-deckers was of the synchromesh type and therefore should be easier to use than the constant-mesh box on the KSW. However, I personally never noticed the difference. To me, it always seemed that one was searching for a gear in a bowl of porridge! This was probably due to the fact that the gear box was half-way down the bus with a lot of linkage mitigating the directness of a gear box situated next to the (front) engine. The gears on the newer MWs were marginally easier to find than those on the LS single-deckers. I never really came to terms with these single-deckers or enjoyed driving them. I imagine that if you drove them all the time, like the OMO drivers, you got used to them and probably got to know the characteristics of the individual buses.

I spent a happy two weeks working all day at the driving school. And, what is more, I got paid for it! This was some very welcome extra income for me as a student. Then I returned to college for my final term. There I finished my studies and passed my final examinations. At the end of June 1968 it was time to leave college, be ordained to the ministry of the Church and take up my post as a curate in the Parish of Billericay. But first I had to return to Clacton, complete my driver training and work as a driver for Eastern National for three months.

When I returned to the driving school another Inspector was in charge. He was a very patient and encouraging person and a good teacher. On the afternoon of the Friday of my first week back we had to go to Colchester for a driving test for one of the learners. There were three of us on the bus with the inspector and the third man asked for permission to go home when we got to Colchester. I therefore went upstairs and made myself scarce while the remaining learner driver took his driving test, which he passed. Then he went off somewhere. When he had gone, the inspector came upstairs and said to me: "The examiner says that he will give you your driving test now if you like". Of course I agreed and, at the shortest possible notice, on a Friday afternoon in June 1968 I took my PSV test in Colchester. And much to my surprise and relief I passed. I was now authorised to drive every kind of Public Service Vehicle in the United Kingdom: whether they were fitted with constant-mesh, semi-automatic or automatic gear-boxes, or whether they were single-deck or double-deck and up to the, then, maximum length of thirty-six foot. I then drove 2331 back to Clacton with a new degree of confidence.

I had passed my Public Service Vehicle (PSV) driving test on the Friday *[in June 1968]* and on Saturday morning I began my first duty at Clacton Bus Station as a driver. The first service that I worked on was the 110 (Holland-on-Sea to Jaywick Sands via Holland Road and the Hospital). This was the most tightly timed of all the town services with only two minutes turn round time at each end. However the regular bus was probably the most suitable at Clacton Garage: that is No. 2701 (81 TVX). This was, I believe, the only batch of Bristol FLFs in the fleet with the four-speed gear-box.

As when I had been a conductor at Clacton in 1965, there were three rotas; the regular crew rota, the seasonal crew rota and the OMO rota. As then, the seasonal rota covered nearly all of the town services. However the Burrsville Circular services (113/114), which had in the past been entirely single-deck and mainly OMO, were now operated by double-deckers and were on the permanent rota. For some reason two seasonal services also seemed to be kept to the permanent rota, these were the 121 'shorts' to Meadow View Camp and the 125 (to Highlands Camp). Another seasonal service, the long-standing 129 (to Valley Farm Camp) seemed to be confined to one-man-operation. Of these, the only service that I worked on overtime was the 125.

After a few days I was put with a regular conductor, who was also a student, and we worked together for the rest of the summer. However when working over-time I sometimes worked with other conductors. On most occasions I signed on at the Bus Station but when working the first bus of the day it was necessary to sign on at Castle Road Garage. This entailed finding the allocated bus and driving it to the Bus Station. This is where another piece of advice from the driving instructor came in. This was that the gear-box would be more difficult to operate when it was cold but, not to worry, be patient and it would soon warm up. I found this to be especially true one morning with UEV 832 (2339) which I think was originally a Chelmsford bus and one that I had probably travelled to work on ten years earlier. It was a good bus. Although slow gear changes and slow progress in traffic might be an embarrassment to a car driver, when driving a bus (or HGV) because it is so big, there is not much that anyone else can do about it if you are taking your time. Thus the slow change of a constant-mesh (crash) gear-box is not really much of a problem, in this respect at least.

Someone, I do not know whether it was driving instructor or fellow driver, told me that it was possible to change gear with a constant-mesh gear-box without using the clutch. However it was important to get the timing and the engine revolutions just right. I tried this at 2300 (11pm) one night on the sea-front coming back from Holland-on-Sea on the last service 112. The bus was a covered top KSW. Much to my own satisfaction it worked beautifully: however I cannot see how one could start a bus from stationary without using the clutch.

The Burrsville (113/114) services were on the permanent rota and I only worked on them on overtime. The occasion that I remember was signing off at about 1400 (2pm) on a Saturday and being asked by the regulator to do a couple of Burrsville Circulars, which I agreed to do: overtime was always welcome. The bus was 2353 (UEV 841) which was a KSW5G that had been delivered to Westcliff soon after the Eastern National take-over. It was one of the first buses delivered in green livery to Southend Garage. I had a soft spot for this bus as I could remember it being delivered to Southend when brand new. As an ex-Southend bus it seemed a little 'livelier' than ones from traditional Eastern National garages. Like many Southend buses it seemed a bit low on its near-side springs but it ran well and the two Burrsville Circulars were an easy way of earning an hour's overtime.

So what about the rest of the bus fleet at Clacton in 1968? Well, all the Bristol K5Gs and the Leyland PD1 open-toppers had gone. They had been replaced by KSW5Gs and Lodekkas of both the LD5G rear-entrance type and front entrance FLFs with Gardner 6LW or Bristol BVW engines. Nearly all the Walton services (107) were operated by FLFs. The town services were mainly in the hands of KSWs and LD5Gs.

There were also two KSW5G open-toppers which had been converted from the WNO batch of 'staggered seat' vehicles. As with all Eastern National engineering work, they had been rebuilt to a very high standard to which the preserved examples testify forty years later. The open-toppers were used on the sea front service (112). When it rained and in the evenings they were usually replaced by closed-top vehicles if possible: these could be other KSWs or a Lodekka of some kind (LD or FLF). The open-toppers were the best of the KSWs to drive: probably because they were only used for less than six months each year and then not in bad weather. One of these buses was an exceptionally smooth running vehicle. The engine ran 'as sweet as a nut'. There was none of the roar and clatter usually associated with Gardner 5LW engines: it was silky smooth. On one occasion it reached 39mph on the straight section of road between Butlin's and the Three Jays on the 112 service. That was flying for a KSW5G!

On one occasion I took over an FLF Lodekka on a town service which was doing a reasonable impression of steam engine: the radiator was in need of water. The radiator cap on most Bristol's at this time was a flap held in position by a smaller flap. I had been told that the way to open them safely when hot was to run past it and give it a thump as I went past. Thus the flap would open but I would be out of the way if any hot water gushed out. This I did and, much to my surprise, it worked. I then poured three (!) cans of water into the radiator. Clearly the water level had not been checked for some time.

The only non-Bristol vehicle was the ex-Moores Commer 'Avenger' with TS3 engine and Yeates 'Riviera' coach body (102, 7652 VW). This coach reputedly had very heavy steering. The noise of the engine reminded me of the LS bus 400 (476 BEV) which was fitted with a Rootes TS3 engine as an experiment when new. I seem to remember that 400 had gained the nick-name 'The Banger'. I think that 400 was always a Chelmsford bus but turned up in Clacton from time to time on service 53 (Clacton to Tilbury Ferry). I travelled home from Chelmsford to Clacton on 400 in 1958 and experienced the rasping sound of the TS3 engine for over two hours. 400 was fitted with a Gardner 5HLW engine in 1960. I gather that the Foden two-stroke diesel engine has a similar reputation for noise: as indeed do GM Detroit diesels.

Although the other buses were standard Tilling group examples, besides the open-toppers and 2700, there was one other bus that merits mention. It was, I think, 2364 (VNO 859, now preserved). This was one of the three Bristol KSW5Gs built with platform doors for the long, ex-Hicks, Braintree to London service (322). These three buses also had staggered seating upstairs which they retained. I imagine that the idea of open-toppers with platform doors seemed to be a strange idea to the 'powers that be' at Eastern National at the time. Or perhaps they did not need any more open-toppers. Anyway, it was a nice bus but a bit sluggish which was probably due to the fact that the platform doors added about half of a ton to the weight. Driving one of these buses on the 322, the forty-seven miles from Braintree to London, especially in the London traffic, must have required a good deal of patience but the driver could be sure that it would get there!

A few examples might help to illustrate the surprises and experiences in store for a summer bus driver: in the 1960s at least. One day, when the Clacton carnival was on, as usual, the procession brought the centre of the town to a standstill. The buses were in the wrong positions at the wrong time. In my case we ended up at Fernwood Avenue at Holland-on-Sea at about the same time as the other bus on the 112 (Sea Front) service. The schedules side of my brain calculated that if we went back to Clacton straightaway we would be there in time to work our following departure to Holland-on-Sea. Thus we left the other bus to work the service from Holland to Jaywick Sands. We turned the destination indicator to 'PRIVATE', something that we rarely did, and hastened back to Clacton Bus Station. We pulled into the bus station and received puzzled and worried looks from the regulator. In those days it was unusual for Eastern National buses to run 'dead' (light) anywhere: especially those engaged on Clacton town services. I explained my thinking to him and he accepted my idea whole-heartedly. We then returned to Holland-on-Sea as a number 112.

The town services in Clacton were much the same as in 1965. Most were on a simple hourly or half-hourly headway. The exception was the 121 (Highfield Park to Jaywick Sands) which had three buses each hour on a roughly twenty minute headway. One bus each hour ran via Clacton Railway Station and took a few minutes longer than the direct service via Old Road. These extra minutes were the reason why the service was not exactly every twenty minutes. After 1900 hours (7pm), all the buses on the 121 ran direct via Old Road. However one evening I forgot and on the first bus after 1900 I went via the Station to the consternation of some of the passengers! I wondered why it was so quiet at the Railway Station!

One of the rarely appreciated skills of a bus driver at a garage like Clacton or Rock Ferry is the wide route knowledge that is required. This is more than just knowing the local geography of North Essex, in the case of Clacton, or the Wirral and North Wales in the case of Rock Ferry. Most routes divert into a village or a town housing estate on their way to their destination. This can be especially true of school journeys and works services. My children told me that on the highly developed school-bus network in Bolton, it was not unusual for the driver to ask the school children for directions. This is in no way a criticism of Bolton drivers as I imagine this may well be the case in other towns.

As I have already mentioned, at Clacton Garage in the summer, seasonal crews were sometimes offered overtime on routes covered by the permanent rota. This usually entailed working half of a shift. In the summer most of the permanent rota was taken up with the longer distance services, as the town services were nearly all worked by the seasonal crews. While overtime was always welcome to seasonal crews, many of whom were students; it was a definite advantage if you, as the driver, knew where to go!

The overtime on the permanent rota which I did was mainly on the shorter distance services such as the 101A to Point Clear and the 101B to

St. Osyth Beach. Both of these services were worked by single-deckers; usually the older LS type as against the MW. This involved the usual game, for me at least of 'find the gear'. In the event I managed to cope without any great disasters or embarrassment.

The other out of town route that we tended to work on overtime was the 107 to Walton-on-Naze. I only worked the direct journeys but some went via Kirby-le-Soken and some went via Ashes Corner. Some journeys were also extended beyond Walton Bus Station to The Naze. Most of these services were worked by FLF Lodekkas but I worked one early morning journey with one of the older LD5G Lodekkas.

Two incidents come to mind when writing about the 107 route. First, late in the morning, there were two services from Walton that ran into Clacton within five minutes of each other. We were on one of these journeys but by some chance we arrived at Clacton out of order. Both buses were left on the stand for Walton. However the conductor of the other bus left his ticket machine on the bus ready to work back to Walton. When he and his driver returned from a quick visit to the canteen, their bus was gone: and so had the conductor's ticket machine! I do not know how they resolved that problem as it was time for us to go home.

The other event was caused by one of the activities that was part of Walton Carnival Week. On the evening of one day the Walton services were disrupted by a pram race (!) which had taken over the streets of Walton. My conductor and I finished our shift just before 2100 (9pm) and my conductor lived at Walton. He wanted to get home and so did a reasonable sized queue of people waiting at the Walton stand in Clacton Bus Station. All the buses on the Walton service were trapped in Walton. My conductor and I therefore offered to work a 107 service to Walton on the understanding that he would get off at Walton and I would bring the bus back to Clacton 'dead' (light). The regulator, who happened to be the instructor who put me through my driving test, readily agreed with our suggestion. He allocated us an FLF Lodekka from the half-dozen that were parked in the middle of the bus station and promised us two hours overtime. So off we went to Walton with a good load of happy passengers.

On our way out of Clacton, between the Railway Station and Holland Road School, we passed all four buses on the Walton service making their way to Clacton, having escaped from Walton. Some of the drivers gave us very strange looks! Having arrived at Walton Bus Station, the most difficult thing was explaining to the waiting passengers why I could not take them to Clacton! I then had a leisurely evening drive back to Clacton across the Holland Marshes and parked the FLF in the middle of the bus station.

One Saturday lunch-time we worked one of the infrequent and irregular journeys on service 102 to Brightlingsea. I knew that the route ran via Great Bentley and that it was necessary to take the second lane on the right after the dip in the main road after St. Osyth. This I did successfully and the journey there and back was uneventful. The vehicle allocated to the working was an FLF Lodekka. Great Bentley Green makes the claim to being the second largest village green in England, covering 43 acres. I imagine that most people who live there and use public transport to get to Clacton or Colchester use the regular electric train service. There was an equally irregular service from Great Bentley to Colchester (77/77A). The other service that served Brightlingsea was the regular 78 to Colchester. At one time there was a British Rail branch line from Wivenhoe. This closed in June 1964 as part of the Beeching cuts. The only time that I travelled on it, it was worked by a J15: happy days! *[The J15 was a very large class of 0-6-0 tender locos introduced by the Great Eastern Railway which lasted through LNER days well into the BR era]*.

The two main trunk routes were from Clacton to Colchester. They were the 19/19A (to Southend) and the 53 (to Tilbury Ferry). Clacton Garage shared the workings between Clacton and Colchester with Colchester Garage. Later on Lodekkas had taken over. Interestingly it is one of the services that I cannot remember being worked by a Bristol KSW. In the late 1950s, the General Manager of Eastern National, Mr Richards, had a vision of making the 19/19A like a Green Line route and thus the double-deckers were replaced by LS and MW single-deckers. I imagine the crews appreciated this especially on the quiet evening journeys. Anyway, by 1968 these services were worked by Bristol FLF double-deckers.

In many cases on the 19/19A and the 53, half of a shift consisted of two round trips to Colchester. However, as far as I can remember, when we worked service 19, we just worked the last round trip: the 9pm (2100) from Clacton and the 10.15pm (2215) back. Throughout the day service 19/19A left Colchester on the hour but the last journey left at 10.15pm and ran via the recently opened Essex University at Wivenhoe Park to provide a slightly later service for the students. I knew where the University was but I had never been inside the gates. In the event we found our way inside the gates all right but, in the dark, I could not see the stands very well and pulled up at the wrong stand. As far as I know no harm was done as we were the only bus in sight and we did not leave anyone behind.

The service 19/19A route to Colchester was about sixteen and a half miles long. For most of the way it followed the A133 which has some good straight sections on it between Weeley, Frating and Elmstead Market as well as a dual carriageway section between Elmstead Market and the Wivenhoe junction. Service 19/19A was one of the routes where the fifth gear on the FLFs came into its own. With a running time of 55 minutes, it was fairly easily timed for most of the day. The busiest section of the route was between Weeley and Clacton. The 53, on the other hand, was more tightly timed. It followed a route of about a mile longer than the 19 and had the same running time. It also diverted into St. Osyth and Wivenhoe, and the only relatively fast section of the route was the main road between Thorington Cross and Wivenhoe. My experience of the 53 was to work two return journeys one evening in August: the 6.30 pm and 8.30 pm from Clacton.

The 53 and 51 had an interesting history. The 51 was the service to Harwich and in my time at Eastern National it was worked as a separate service between Colchester and Harwich by Dovercourt and Colchester Garages. Service 51 had been created in 1930 by combining the services originally numbered 17A (Harwich to Colchester), 5 (Colchester to Chelmsford) and 42 (Chelmsford to Tilbury Ferry). The 51 was publicised as 'The straight line across Essex by Eastern National – Coast to Coast' (as illustrated on page 10 of *"The Years between 1909–1969: Vol.2 The Eastern National Story from 1930"* by Crawley, MacGregor and Simpson). That straight line had however been broken in April 1964 when the route was curtailed to run just between Colchester and Harwich, but a new "straight line" was created the following year when the 51 was combined with the 70 (Colchester to Braintree, ex Moores) and 310 (Braintree to Bishops Stortford) as the 70, Harwich to Bishops Stortford, from 11th April 1965. *[Meanwhile, the number 51 was appropriated for a new Chelmsford town service that started in June 1965.]*

However I would think that it would be true to say that for most of its history the main service was the 53 to Clacton. It is also true to say that, for most of its history, the through workings were operated by single-deckers of one sort or another. In my experience they were LS/MW under floor engined vehicles but before that they were Bristol L5Gs. This was, I think, because the section through Laindon and over Langdon Hills was deemed not suitable for double-deckers. When Basildon New Town was developed in the 1950s and 1960s, the roads were improved and the route became suitable for double-deck operation. This would have brought good savings for the company as the section between Chelmsford and Colchester was heavily duplicated to meet the needs of traffic and, I imagine, also because Moore Brothers of Kelvedon ran a competing service over this section of the route. Between them the two companies provided a half-hour frequency between Chelmsford and Colchester.

For the enthusiast and drivers bored with Bristol buses, service 53 held other delights. After Eastern National took over Moore Brothers in 1963 the Moore's Colchester to Chelmsford service was absorbed into service 53. This meant that Kelvedon Garage had a share in the working of service 53. The occasional delights were in the form of ex-Moores or 'ordered by Moores' 30 foot long Guy Arab IV double-deckers with Massey 67 seater low-bridge bodies. I never saw one of the two Northern Counties bodied ones on service 53. These buses were fitted with Gardner 5LW engines. In the excellent book *'The Colours of Greater Manchester'* (by Michael Eyre and Peter Greaves and published by Capital Transport), a batch of Daimler CVG5s with Crossley bodies of 1949 are described as 'the most underpowered buses ever'. These Moore Brothers Guys are also surely strong contenders for this title as well as many buses in the ex-Tilling

Group companies. Eastern National's KSW5Gs with platform doors come to mind as well as Eastern Counties many Gardner 5LW powered Lodekkas also fitted with platform doors.

In Brian Everitt's book 'The Story of Moore Brothers Kelvedon, Essex', he says: "Some reduction of weight (on 30 foot Guy Arabs) was achieved by the use of fibreglass instead of metal for the bonnet top, front wings and concealed radiator panel, but increased power was desirable for this larger bus and therefore Guy Motors decided they would not offer the 5-cylinder Gardner engine for this chassis version. However, it is interesting to note that an exception was made for Moore Bros. and the five-cylinder engine was fitted, principally because of their services operating over flat terrain".

On the one occasion that I saw one of these buses at Clacton on the service 53, it was one of the two that had been ordered by Moores' and delivered to Eastern National and to Eastern National specification (581/2 AOO, 1049/50, later 2018/9). This meant that the seats were covered with Eastern National pattern moquette and the buses were fitted with Tilling type 'T' destination indicator at the front (only). The Clacton driver who was taking over this bus, who also happened to be an OMO driver and therefore was on over-time, looked delighted in having such an interesting bus to drive to Colchester. Whether he was just as delighted when he got there, I cannot say!

Early in September 1968, on my last Friday as a driver at Clacton Garage, my conductor and I were asked to cover the second half of a duty that involved the 6.30pm (1830) to Ipswich and 8.30pm (2030) return plus the 10.30pm (2230) to Thorpe Green and return. As I have mentioned before, service 123 to Ipswich was a long route of 29 miles with a running time of 1 hour and 45 minutes. It diverted from the direct road to Ipswich to take in Bradfield on its way to Mistley and Manningtree. Then after Brantham it went off the main road at Tattingstone to run through Holbrook. Neither my conductor nor I were completely sure of the route but we thought that we could cope between us if we were allocated a single-decker. The normal bus was an FLF Lodekka which, from the driving point of view, I would have preferred. Such was the urgency that we were given an MW single-decker and successfully navigated our way to Ipswich. At Ipswich Railway Station we caught up with an Eastern Counties single-decker and followed it to the bus station. Fortunately we found the Clacton stand successfully and after a visit to the canteen returned to Clacton without incident. At 10.30pm we returned the way that we had just come on the short working to Thorpe Green and back on service 106. For some reason all the short workings to Thorpe Green were included in the 106 service timetable although they covered exactly the same route as the 104 and the 123.

The next day I worked my rostered shift on the seasonal rota and signed off as a bus driver for the last time. Thus ended one of the dreams of a lifetime: I had been a bus driver!

I must conclude this part of my memoirs by eating a large portion of 'humble-pie'! Throughout these memoirs I have been less than complimentary about buses fitted with Gardner 5LW engines. However my experience as a driver has brought about a sneaking regard and affection for them! In fact the Bristol KSW5G with low-bridge body is one of my all time favourite buses. This is partly because it is the type of bus that I passed my PSV test on and partly because I preferred the higher driving position than the more 'laid back' position of the Bristol Lodekka. It also had a relatively simple gear-box.

In 1958 a group of parishioners from St. James Church in Hadleigh came to Clacton for the induction of their old Rector, the Revd. Roger Lewis, as the new Vicar of St. Paul's Church in Clacton. Their transport was a Bristol KSW5G of Southend Garage: one of the EJN batch. Rather cheekily, I said to the driver: "How do you think that you will get up Market Hill, Maldon?". He answered: "Once I get her into her crawler gear she will go anywhere!". I am sure that he was right!

RTC

Conducting at Southend

Yes this is about Conductor Harper, but not the antics of Jack Harper, the conductor-come-crew mate of Driver Butler (Reg Varney) in the venerable TV series! However I did work on the buses most often used for 'Luxton & District' in the TV show (Eastern National's FLF6LX Lodekkas 2917 & 2930) on several occasions. I even once set the destination blinds to 'Cemetery Gates/ 11' at Wood Green just for fun! But, there was no Inspector Blakey saying, "I'm going to get you Butler!" but there is still plenty to tell, nonetheless…

It was on a train to St. Pancras in the autumn of 1973, returning from an interview at the University of Leicester, that I made an important decision: to go on and get a university education, but to defer my entry for at least a year. The official reason was to gain some experience of the world from other than a school student's perspective and to save some money for college, both of which were true. However, and perhaps more importantly, it was also to fulfill a boyhood ambition while I still had the chance: to work on the buses! And so it was the following July (1974), after completing my 'A'-levels at the South East Essex VIth form college in Thundersley, that I found myself in the first day of Conductor's School at Eastern National's (EN) Southend (SD) depot.

A Conductor's Life

On the surface of it, I had supposed being a bus conductor was little more than collecting some fares and ringing a few bells! But through the instructor, Inspector Kennedy, my classmates and I soon learned that there was more to it than that. We were soon reading fare tables and timetables, practicing making change (quickly), operating our Setright Speed ticket machines, understanding duty cards and completing waybills. Of course, how to ensure the safe operation the bus along the way was stressed as the number one concern.

The week passed very quickly. Before my fellow students and I knew it, we were being issued our own ticket machine boxes and uniforms. The latter consisted of the both the heavier black serge (winter) uniform of trousers and jacket with gold stripes along the trouser seams and jacket pockets, collar and cuffs, and the lighter olive/green (summer) cotton "dust" jacket, which I actually wore most of the time. The winter uniform was replaced by the (actually) more comfortable, but less distinctive blue-grey National Bus Company (NBC) uniform later on.

My First Duty

However the real training began the following week with my supervised 'road' training. I had been teamed up with Fred Matthews and his driver Eric Buisson. In fact, Eric's wife, Rene, was also a fellow student in the same Conductor's school, but more of that later. As was typical for most crews at the time, we boarded an empty 'Wood Green' on its way to Southend's Central Bus Station, or 'Scab' as it was endearingly known, based on its destination code, SCB, to take over a mid-morning 6 to Newington Ave.

The entire journey was a blur, with more and more people boarding between SCB and Victoria (Vic) Circus (SVC as I recall). Try as I might, I was unable to leave the lower saloon. Fred tended to the upstairs and, apart from my honour of ringing the first 'ding-ding' to signal our departure from SCB, he rang the remaining bells. I was somewhat familiar with the major destinations along Southchurch Rd, but those along Hamstel Rd and Newington Ave were new territory for me. I'm pretty certain that most of the tickets I issued had, at best, the completely the wrong fare stages on them! Fred made sure I completed the first line of my waybill and I managed to catch my breath.

The return journey to Kent Elms Corner (EKE) wasn't much better. There were some pretty severe turns along the way and I was being bounced around as I hadn't found my 'legs' yet! I needed to develop the fine balancing act between issuing tickets and negotiating a narrow gangway on a moving bus, with a heavy bag of change on one side and a hefty ticket machine on the other. Fortunately it was something that came relatively quickly. From Kent Elms we had to go back all the way to Newington Ave, return to Kent Elms before heading only as far as SCB to hand over to the next crew. After the hectic pace of the cross-town morning 6's, a hard-earned lunch was in order. Then we were off on a circuit to Canvey.

During the course of the next few days, my knowledge of the both the route system and the history expanded rapidly, taking in the 3, 22/A, 25/A, 27, 29A, 61 and of course the longer distance 2 (to Grays) and 251: the 2 hour 40 minute (one–way) run into Wood Green in North-East London. The most notable omission was the 5 from Shoebury to Canvey, but I guess they figured the 3 and 27 would cover it! During the course of the week Eric and Fred shared much of the fabled "lore" of the SD depot with me: the conductor's ultimate days work – two Wood Greens and a Grays, which would have covered the best part of two-and-half shifts, or an entire working day!; X10 and 151/251 slashes – loading up a entire bus full of passengers and running off timetable to or from London Victoria or Wood Green; the now defunct cross-town 28/29 'figure of 8.' There was a fondness for these past (glory?) days as both these men recounted their little tit-bits and embellishments. Eric had also spent several summers as coach driver too, so he recounted many of those (antics) stories as well.

I also learned that my routine would consist of alternating between a regular schedule of a 'week' (any five days in a row) of early's, starting mostly before 10:00 am, and a week of late's, starting after 1:00 pm or so. The schedule was arranged such that once every several weeks you'd have a long weekend: finishing on a Thursday and not starting until the following Tuesday. This was, of course counter-balanced with changing over from an early week on Saturday, to a late week on a Sunday! Most of the time there was a day or two off between the different weeks. Also, within any given week, each day's duty was different. You would know the day before what the following day's duty would be. Adding in overtime, particularly on the late weeks, always made life extremely interesting. On those occasions you might only know that you needed to be at depot by 10:30 am, to be available to pick something up. Other times you would know that it was for a specific half-shift or whatever. It made for a varied and interesting work schedule. And, of course, plenty of overtime pay! Interspersed with these regular duties were the occasional "spares," when you would just show up with no specifically assigned work to cover, in case someone else didn't show up because they were sick or whatever. These "spare" times could be for only an hour or two at the beginning or end of a shift, to a half or whole shift.

I was also getting used to the different buses we worked on too: primarily the open-backed 27 feet LD Lodekka seating 60 (33 up/27 down), and the two different configurations of the longer, front-entrance FLF's: the standard 30 feet long, FLF with its rearward facing staircase and manual gearbox, versus the 31 foot semi-automatic version with a forward facing staircase and a luggage pen downstairs. Both seated 70 but in different layouts: the former were 38/32, as opposed to the latter being 40/30. During my training I never did work on a KSW, by then only used on seafront duties, or on either of ENOC's two FS Lodekka's: I think only one of them was assigned to SD anyway, and unlike all the other LD's, they had a completely flat floor downstairs.

I also learnt some of the trickier operating procedures too. I successfully changed my first ticket roll on a moving bus, without having it unfurl along the entire lower deck. I had to wait for much later on for that to happen! There were several interesting manoeuvres at the end of routes too, to turn the bus around for the return journey. None more so than the 22A where the bus was reversed around blind corners at both Lower Hockley/Church Road, and Lifstan Way/Woodgrange Drive. The latter was actually into a side-street just beyond Lifstan Way. However, before I knew it, my week of training was over. I had just about found my legs; it was time to go it alone!

Solo at last!

Well, almost solo: I had my PSV licence (FF30535? if I recall correctly), my ticket machine with box and a well worn leather cash bag, which was nice and supple and easy on the hands. All I needed was a driver! My first driver, or 'mate,' was Bill Bailey: a veteran of the Westcliff Omnibus Company, and was a member of the Black Cat gang. Although he never really explained who or what they were, he did still have the tattoo on his hand and seemed to be genuinely proud of it! He was a driver from the old school, although he could get a little impatient when driving, particularly in heavy traffic, which he would have seen get much worse over the years. It wasn't the easiest of partnerships, but there was no denying he was an interesting character, with a long history as a busman and was particularly engaging when he talked about the 'old' days.

My first duty was the gruelling 'first Cambridge' (not to the University City, but the Cambridge Hotel, Shoebury/22), which started around 4:50 AM. Fortunately my Dad decided he would get up early with me to drive me to SD, and wish me luck on my first day. So it was with a deal of trepidation that I climbed up the front of my first Lodekka, adjusted the then standard T-shaped destination blinds:

Shoeburyness Cambridge Hotel 22

I descended, walked around, hit the emergency door button and boarded; set up my trusty Setright ticket machine, fully loaded with a brand new ticket roll; checked my float of change in my bag; studied the duty card one last time; stowed my ticket machine box in the cubby; and rapped the bulkhead window with a coin, twice. Bill glanced back through the bulkhead window, smiled, nodded, and out we rolled. I was finally on my way!

Unlike most 22 duties, which involved a Southend-Hullbridge-Shoebury-Southend circuit, this one started out from Southend towards Shoebury first, making a complete circuit, before handing over to the next crew back in Southend after a second departure from the Cambridge Hotel. It was a long and pretty gruelling duty since it started early, picking up some early commuters out of Shoebury, hitting a solid commuter rush out of Hullbridge, for Rayleigh Station, as well as picking up a fairly heavy load of office workers into Southend, and was still busy on the second leg out of Shoebury, back into Southend, again.

I must say that working with Bill did have some plus points. The first was that with an FLF, Bill was easily able to monitor the passengers loading and unloading on the platform, without out me having to give the "double bell" signal to depart from every stop. A blessing on that first busy morning!

Secondly, he was the master of the double de-clutch down the Lodekka gearbox. It was his absolute joy on 22/A's to be going full pelt down the Hullbridge Road, in overdrive, and then have to change down, double de-clutching through the box as we approached the sharp turn at Watery Lane into Hullbridge. I will never forget the sound of the engine roaring multiple times as he negotiated the gearbox down to second to take the corner! My job was to make sure Bill knew that no one wanted to alight from the bus at any of the stops along that stretch of road. An affirmative nod after we left Rawreth Lane was usually sufficient. This early trip into Hullbridge was, of course, the perfect opportunity for this!

Thirdly, Bill wanted to know the 'car' numbers for each day's duty. Each day the buses were allocated to a car number, corresponding to those on the individual duty cards for each shift. They were shown on 'the Board', together with any vehicles that were spare (unallocated). So on one day Car #8 was 2793, the next day it was 2848 and so on. So, with our car numbers from the Duty card in hand, he would check 'the Board' to see which buses we had. Like most drivers, Bill had his favourite vehicles that he liked to drive. The board was maintained by Derek (Ball?): I never knew what his actual job title was! However, in the event that Derek was off sick, on holiday and so forth, Bill was one of the backup men for setting up the Board too. So he also understood when the various vehicles would be in the depot or out on service. So, unlike most drivers it seems, he would change the assignments if one of his favourites was still available to take out that day!

Lastly, I was expected to buy the tea! I can only suppose that this tradition grew up in the in the hey-days when a conductor was always able to collect enough 'spare' change for this from large volumes of short journey passengers at busy times handing over their fares as they got off, and not necessarily all receiving a ticket in exchange. In these latter days, there were many fewer such opportunities. Although I do recall on a late afternoon 22, taking a full load of evening commuters out of Rayleigh Station, with an Inspector on board. By the time we left the High Street, it was standing room only downstairs, but I had managed to clear all those fares by Trinity Road. However, the upstairs passengers were also now beginning to get off, and just handing me money, with the Inspector watching me on the platform. I rapidly started to count the money into my bag, and issued a ticket to him for the total amount. He smiled, checked it, clipped it and put it the used ticket bin. He then leaned across and poured a handful of change he had also collected, while I was working away from the platform downstairs, winked and got off at the next stop! More often than not, however, I paid out of my own float, if only to keep the tradition going.

I was actually very surprised just how many routes had cafes at, or close to their ends. The 22 was the favourite: it had cafes at both the Anchor in Hullbridge and the Cambridge Hotel. And, indeed, by the time, we reached the Cambridge for the second time that first morning, a warm cuppa was certainly needed. Furthermore, as we turned over the bus at SCB, and hopped on a 'CAR to GAR', a hearty breakfast was most definitely in order!

Car to Gar

That was the Duty card instruction to return the bus back to the garage, empty and out of service. Its reciprocal was of the above mentioned 'CAR to SCB'. This was where most services originated/terminated in central Southend, with the notable exception (for EN crews at any rate) of short 25's, which had a brief layover in Southend's "Deeping," the underground bus stop below the Shopping Centre at Vic Circus. So there was a constant stream of crews, drivers and buses plying back and forth between SD and SCB. Whilst a nice stroll down the High Street was great in good weather, at other times the privacy and shelter of an "empty" bus, as opposed to one in service, was the preferred choice. There were plenty to choose from every hour: two 2's, 11, 19, two 251's, and 400. Also, although I can't fully recall now, but I think there were some short 25's, 27's, 29's, and 61's as well, particularly early morning and late evening as those duties started and ended. In any case it was always a common courtesy to see if there was any one waiting to go back to SD, or, to make an announcement in the Canteen, which inevitably meant there were several others riding to or from SCB with you. I've already mentioned the short 25's with their Deeping layover, but the other main change over point was in the SD depot itself, where crews would relieve each other on the longer Canvey services (3/5), since they didn't pass through SCB.

This also brings to mind a curiosity about how folks talked about the different routes we operated. In town services were almost always referred to by their numbers (6, 25, 29) and not their destinations. No one was doing a round of Leigh Churches (short 25's), or Newington Ave's (6/A), or perhaps even more whimsically "Kent Elmsies," although that might have been fun! Curiously, the 61 was often referred to as a Sutton Cemetery! Whereas, for the longer services, it was much more common for the destination to be used, instead of a number: a Hullbridge (22), a Grays (2), a Wood Green or London (251) and so on. These would often include some kind of qualifier too: first, morning, mid-day, afternoon, late, last and so on. There was also some (albeit readily understood) ambiguity involved in this. The first Shoebury was a 22, not a 3 or a 5: these would have been the first East Beach or Blackgate Road, but I can't remember actually ever doing either.

Having been refreshed with a hearty breakfast Bill and I were back out for the second half of our shift. I don't remember now what that was, although I suspect it was a round or two of short town services (6/6A, short 25/25A or 29A), but it was over very early in the afternoon. I had survived my first solo day. It was time to go home for a good rest and to relax before the next day's work. Fortunately this was a later start so I could get the bus in. In hindsight, I really wasn't ready for that first week and did not take on any overtime. That would shortly follow, once I'd got into a regular daily routine.

Having found my legs and learned the "basics" of what it meant to be a Conductor, I found myself quickly falling into the daily routine of my new found life in the depot. Despite the variation of shifts each day and each week, there was a relaxed cadence to the work which became both pleasant and comfortably familiar. There were also plenty of opportunities for overtime, which I eagerly took on most occasions. However, no matter what any particular day's work was, at some point it became almost inevitably centred on the canteen!

"Weak and Sweet!"

That cry is forever burned in my memory! A procession of drivers and conductors would push open the swing doors to the canteen and call for a weak tea with two sugars. Often it was directed at no one in particular, sometimes the canteen staff would respond, sometimes it would be a fellow driver or conductor in the queue. It still amazes me the amount of sugar we all consumed! On a good day, with overtime, I could have as many as 8–9 cups of tea, each with two sugars! In fact, it got to be so much that I started to drink tea without the sugar after a while, and still do to this day!

Since, everyone worked different duties every day, it was easy to meet up and chat or eat with pretty much anyone and everyone every couple of days or so. This was especially true if you were working overtime shifts as well, which were plentiful at the time. For me it was a good way to earn that extra money for college, so I frequently took the opportunity when it was available.

There was almost always a running card game going in one corner or the other. It was called Kalooki and was a variant of Rummy. People were constantly joining and leaving, including my 'mate' Bill, and it seemed that some amount of money was changing hands too! Fred, my training conductor, was another one of the regulars at the card table, as was his Mum.

A Family Affair

While Bill was off playing cards, I would spend my time with others I had met, and worked with. There were several younger lads, conductors mostly, who hung around together in the canteen: Johnny Corder, Dave Molyneux, Steve Pettit, Johnny Allen as well as some of their younger drivers too: Tim Hutchins (I recall that his conductor was another Steve), Alan (Clark – I think, although I could be getting that confused with the lead singer of the Hollies or an Inside Right at Leeds United!), Ray Allen, Phil Brochen and several more. Although there was an obvious trend: many of the conductors were becoming drivers, and rapidly changing to (the then so called, and now politically incorrect) One Man Operation (OMO) duties, but many of them would still 'crew' for overtime.

It was also a family place, literally as well as figuratively. I have already mentioned Fred and his Mum, often playing cards together. Eric was now crewing with his wife, Rene, who I trained with. Their daughter, Denise, was dating Johnny Corder at the time. There were the Embersons: Jack and his wife were a crew; and their son, Dave, was a 400 driver.

Additionally, and one of my favourites, was Joyce, who was certainly like a 'mother' to all of us "young 'uns' ". Joyce was instantly recognisable. She was tall, thin, and dark-haired, and she wore white gloves to keep her hands clean from handling the money. She explained lots of the other 'operational' rules I needed to know, which weren't covered in my training, namely: Twirlies, Lurkers, Scratchers (more on these later) and more besides.

Although the canteen was many things to many people, it was mostly a noisy place. But every now and then even that was shattered by a booming "winter's 'ere!" as either George or Bill (Winters), two of the OMO drivers (not related) entered, followed by the inevitable call: "weak and sweet!" However it was also a place where you could find peace and respite if you needed, when necessary.

He ...

Unless, of course 'he' joined you! 'He' had been to Australia. I assume 'he' went out on the 'passage' in the late Fifties/early Sixties, when for around 20-quid the Aussie government would welcome you with open arms to go and live in Wogga-Wogga, or somewhere else equally forsaken. I had the pleasure of visiting there myself many years later on business (not Wogga-Wogga!, but Sydney and Melbourne) and can easily understand the attraction. I can also easily imagine why many Brits became homesick and turned into "Whinging Poms," reciting a laundry list of things that were wrong, missing, different, bad or whatever about Australia, much to the chagrin of the locals.

'He' had clearly come back! Too many things must have been wrong, missing, different, bad or whatever. However, since doing so, 'he' had now become the opposite: a reformed Whinging Pom! 'He' could now recite a laundry list of things that were right, present, better, good or whatever about Australia, much to the chagrin of the listener: who was, on more than one occasion, me! Sometimes you wondered why the heck 'he' came back, although it was entertaining to watch him engage someone else in this conversation, especially since you were NOT the target!

And then there was Trevor! Trevor was a very flamboyant, extroverted character with mostly dyed (I always assumed) sandy-blond hair. I remember picking him up on more than one occasion at the Prittlewell Bell. As was fairly customary, when the conductor was working away from the platform, he boarded last and gave the signal to go. Seeing me at the far end of the lower deck, full of shoppers on their way into Southend around 10:00 AM or so, he'd bellow some outrageous comment or question to me. Of course I had no choice but to respond with an equally outrageous reply! Then, as we slowed down to an almost stop at the Vic Circus roundabout, he would pop the emergency button to open the doors, and say something loud and outrageous again and disappear off the platform. That, was Trevor!

Although he was ostensibly employed as a conductor, he worked much of the time in the canteen, pouring the inevitable weak and sweet teas, which, by the way, were otherwise as strong and sour as creosote! The canteen fare was very simple and predictable: meat, potatoes and two (cooked to death) veg, fried bacon, eggs, chips, baked beans, bacon or sausage sandwiches and so on. However it did seem to taste that little bit better when Trevor was doing the cooking!

Learning the Ropes

Between riding along with Bill, and listening to Joyce, I quickly learned the ropes, and all the unofficial stuff not covered by my formal training. The first time we did a late, weekend Wood Green, arriving after the EN canteen had closed; Bill jumped out of the cab and signalled me to follow him:

"Where we going?" "You'll see!"

We wandered across to the L.T. Bus Garage and ate there. Bill even received a few nods of acknowledgment, so I surmised he had been doing this for years. One Sunday evening, we walked into the Underground station: Bill pushed open a gate, to the faintest nod of approval from an otherwise completely disinterested ticket collector, and descended down a short stairway into their canteen instead.

Bill also always used to remind me when we were doing late night runs that I should bag up as much money as I could and leave it in the cab with him, instead of in my box in the cubby. It was actually a pretty common and common-sense security practice, although I can personally never ever recall feeling like it was good idea that I had done so. Even so, I did as he suggested.

During my training I had learned that it was the conductor's responsibility to keep time. However, Bill would have none of that! He was driving so he set the pace. He would also try to predict the road conditions ahead, based on many, many years of experience. So we would wait a few extra minutes at Gants Hill, Romford, Brentwood, Wickford, Rayleigh Station, Eastwood Rise, Tarpots, or wherever. Given that we never got written up for running early or arrived anywhere outrageously late, I can only say that he was pretty good judge of things!

Scratchers ...

One thing that both Bill and Joyce were passionate about were Scratchers: those crews who would follow you along a stretch of road and let you do all the work; stopping behind you; never passing. It was always entertaining, for me at any rate, to hear someone vehemently complaining about being scratched down the London Road by some "Hadleigh #$%#$$^%@" (you fill in the blank with your own imagination), or "those %^@#$@@#* Canvey %^%@#$%^&&*" and so forth. People would get so passionate about it!

It seemed very "common" along the London Road, where there were several different depots interworking the (mostly crew-operated) routes (Basildon (BN), Canvey (CY), Hadleigh (HH), SD, as well as the Corporation too), which could become quite congested at times. A sixth form buddy of mine, Les, who was doing the same thing I was, based at Hadleigh, would claim that Southend were worse scratchers than Hadleigh were. However, we could both agree on one thing: Canvey and Basildon were worse than either of us; and the worst of all were the Corporation! (Although, with due respect to our friends at Southend Corporation Transport (SCT), I have to say that I was never scratched by them at all!) I daresay that the SCT crews complained just as vociferously about the ENOC crews in their canteen!

Indeed, I can only ever remember really being scratched once, and I would hardly have noticed except for first the grumbling, then the shouting, followed by the indignant cursing, and finally, the raging epithets emanating from the cab. I was working a Canvey on overtime and it started just after we reached the top of Bread and Cheese Hill (Thundersley) and by the time we got the Elms Hotel (Leigh) I was stunned that driver could even see to drive: the air was so thick and blue in the cab!

Interestingly, I don't recall anybody really complaining of being scratched along the Eastwood Road routes to Rayleigh. I attribute that to several factors: less congestion, more OMO operation (11's, 19's from Chelmsford (CF), and Maldon (MN), Colchester (CR) and Clacton

(CN) respectively), and less interworking on crew routes (mainly SD, with only a few Brentwood (BD) and Wood Green (WG) on 251's and, for only a short distances, HH and the Corporation). I would occasionally see Les and his mate working 23A's, which would always perk up the trip a little, although to my knowledge we never scratched each other along the Eastwood Road, or down the London Road for that matter! I honestly think it was both more of a throwback to earlier times, when it may have been a bigger issue, and more perception than reality, and I really didn't mind the extra work myself anyway.

... Lurkers ...

Frenzied signals were relayed from cab to cab; and from driver to conductor: Watch out, there's a Lurker about! Waiting on the blind side of a shelter, stepped back and obscured by a roadside hedge: an Inspector was on the prowl! They were also referred to as Jumpers and it was a tense moment, as he boarded: Were we on time? Were the blinds set meticulously? Had all the fares been taken? Were they correct? Was it a local man, a Chelmsford Chap or Basildon Bloke? It seemed to me that there were episodes when inspections were frequent, followed by long quiet periods in-between. It always caused a flurry of conversation in the canteen however when they occurred:

"I picked him up at the Carpenters and dropped him at Rayleigh Station"
"Yeah, I got him in Webster's Way"

"We got him on Progress Road going back the other way ..."

I was only ever written up once; on a 6 out of Newington Ave. A young mother had boarded with both a baby in a pram, which I stowed under the stairs, and a toddler. Both children were under the age where they could ride free, so I took the mother's fare and thought no more of it. Eric, one of our local lurkers, must have boarded at the White Horse on Southchurch Rd. By the time I got back downstairs he had checked the lower saloon and was working his way upstairs. He met me back on the platform.

Not bad, but you missed a fare – only one child can ride free," he said as he smiled and handed me the write up. Eric was a kind and jovial man, and always treated me well, whenever he boarded. "Good job young 'un" he called out as he got off at Sutton Road.

Others weren't so fortunate. I recall walking into a very sombre canteen late in the morning one day to learn that, apparently, someone had been dismissed for "irregularities." Whilst several people were trying to ascertain all the details, others were consoling close friends and so on.

We only had a short break, so I told Bill I'd meet him at SCB to pick up our next duty. I wandered down the High Street to get some fish and chips instead of staying in the canteen that day.

There were never too many Lurkers about very early in the morning or last thing at night. They obviously needed time to work their way out from, or back to, base. Whenever I worked the last Hullbridge (which always left me with the issue getting home, since that's where I lived!) several of the local lads and lassies would board at Rayleigh High St after an evening at the one of the Pubs: the Crown, the Half Moon, the Spread Eagle, the Paul Pry, or several of them! I was always pretty slow at getting the fares after letting people board at the High St, Rayleigh Station and sometimes the next stop at the NSS Newsagents. I would start working again after we turned into Downhall Road, knowing I could clear all the fares before reaching Rawreth Lane. By this time the local lads and lassies would have spread themselves around upstairs, taking up the last couple of rows if they were empty, and would be enjoying a smoke.

Sometimes I wouldn't bother them for a fare, although they were always willing to pay: they were always grateful on those occasions.

Once in a while I'd let an old school buddy or two slide by, but on the two times I picked up my Mum going to Rayleigh and from Southend, she was absolutely insistent that I collected her fare. "I'd have to pay if it wasn't you" she said. So I issued her a ticket and left her the money on the counter at home instead!

… and Twirlies

Every weekday morning at around 8:55 AM, marauding packs of Twirlies would gather at bus stops waiting to pounce on the first bus that came along. As the doors jack-knifed open they would simultaneously blind you with the light reflecting off their plastic covered passes and verbally assault you with:

"Am I/Are we/Is it TOO EARLY?"

They were trying to steal a lead on the day and use the half price fare card issued to pensioners for use after 9:00 AM. Most often I would let them on, especially if it was cold or raining, unless we were really full or extra busy: they were only going to pay half price on the bus behind anyway.

The ones that used to annoy me were more subtle: they would just get on and wait until you asked for fares, often waiting until after 9:00 to offer you the money! Apparently, it didn't matter to them that they had boarded before 9:00: "Well it's gone past nine now hasn't it dear?" they would offer by way of explanation. Most of the time it was not worth the argument, but every now and then I'd insist that they would have to pay the full fare, particularly if they had boarded at a stop where the time–tabled departure was clearly before 9:00 AM.

What seemed to confuse them, and, indeed, most passengers for that matter, was how quickly you would learn who had got on where, how much they had paid and where they should get off. I'd say that even on a 'three bell-er (no room left)' I was able to get that right for over 80% of the load. Not bad for a load of 70 seated plus more standing!

Fares please?

The other very surprising item was how quickly the fare structure became ingrained into your head! I always carried my fare table book with me, but rarely used after the first few weeks, unless someone was asking for an "odd" journey: Canvey Newlands to Thorpe Bay; Tottenham Hale to Shotgate, or whatever! There seemed to be four types of passengers when it came to collecting fares:

Those that would simply give you an amount of money, correct or needing change: "22p";

Others who said where they were going, and would have the either the correct money, or need change: "Kent Elms";

Some would say where they wanted to go to and have to be told what the fare was, despite the fact that you suspected (or knew, because they had done the same a week or two before!), they knew what it was: "Vic Circus" "That'll be 12p!"; and

Those you had to ask: "where to luv?"

When it was busy, during rush hours, the former were the most preferable, which was normally the case for the commuters going to the stations! Of course, if they were all piling off at a particular stop and hadn't paid, it was amazing to see how many of them had the correct change and just handed it over! The rest of the time, though, it didn't much matter to me how they asked.

Time for a change

After a few months Bill and I found less to talk about, and it was becoming more frequent for him to cover at the Board as well. I welcomed the breaks. Also, with some newer drivers completing training too, the inevitable happened: Bill and I went our separate ways and I teamed up with my new 'mate', Johnny Corder.

Johnny was a good driver and he learned his craft well. As a conductor he had experienced riding behind the good and the not so good drivers, and that carried forward into his driving as well. We complemented each other more in terms of age and other interests and therefore had plenty to talk about. He knew that we would not be together for a substantial period of time. Even if I hadn't gone onto college as planned, the inevitable march of OMO would have ended the partnership. But for several good months we operated as a real, well blended crew.

For example, if I was working "up-top" two distinct foot stomps above the cab, or on the blind housing were given as the signal to go. Alternatively, two short raps with a coin on the bulkhead glass "inside" were sufficient. Like me, Johnny was also ambivalent to scratchers and the like.

We both liked the steady cadence of a Wood Green although, for a time, there were plenty of road works to contend with around Woodford. I also would try and give Johnny the 'all clear' along the Eastern Avenue section between Newbury Park, through Barley Lane and the Moby Dick roundabout and onto Mawney's roundabout in Romford, so he could wind it up a little!

However, it seems to me, even now, that we had our clearer runs coming back from 'the Smoke', rather than going up. This may have had something to do with the way the SD duties were distributed throughout the day. Conversely, neither of us really liked going to Grays. There were too many turns on and off the A13: into Basildon, Corringham/Stanford-le-Hope and Orsett. It just didn't seem to flow very well.

There was also some unfamiliar territory to cover as well, where Johnny's experience as a conductor came in handy: The open top Seafront 67's now covered a lot of roads no longer travelled by crews anymore, as these had largely been turned over to OMO duties; and there was a schools relief 7 (and a 3) to Shoebury. There were two or three duties with 'long' 29's to Belgrave Rd, and we also had an occasional morning rush hour run into Basildon (14).

However, I'm not sure Johnny was so familiar with where he was going once we got into the industrial estates there either. But we managed to survive, and enjoyed the dead head back to SD. Curiously I never remember a returning evening 14 duty, but I guess that must have been a BN duty, or maybe we just left the passengers there!

There was also a 22C to Runwell Hospital on a Sunday, which I only worked on once. My brother assures me that after that journey I recounted a story of a lady upstairs, sitting in the front bench seat of FLF Lodekka, with an open suitcase, underwear scattered around the seat and the destination blinds housing, changing her bra! I can't recall that at all, which means I have either totally blocked it out of my mind (most wise) or it was reminiscence from someone else that the trip reminded me of. Regardless, if it didn't happen to me, I'd still put money on the fact that it did happen to someone!!

However, as a mark of the operating difficulties and declining ridership, by the time I had returned for my third and final summer in 1976, all these "odd" runs had mostly gone. The two exceptions were one of the long 29's and, of course, the seasonal Seafronts.

So first with Bill, and then with Johnny, I had easily settled in to the daily routine of early and late shifts, with or without overtime. Pretty much every week we were scheduled for at least one Wood Green and one Grays, intermingled with the staple fare (pun intended!) of Hullbridge's, including the Lower Hockley/Dome and Rawreth Lane variants, Canvey's, 6's, 25's, 29's and Sutton Cemetery's.

As easy as it was to get used to the work at hand, I was lucky that most of the journeys passed without any real incident. But, I was dealing with the public, and we were traversing public roads, so there were the inevitable incidents and accidents to deal with. Many were oddities and/or comical. Others were more serious. A lot didn't involve paperwork, but some did!

Incidents and Accidents and Paperwork

One of the first was to discover that the tops of the newly installed traffic island bollards at the junction of Webster's Way and Eastwood Road in Rayleigh, would "pop-off" when clipped by the offside front mudguard of an FLF: we had taken the corner a little too wide!

The most serious incident I had to deal with occurred towards the end of a couple of rounds of 6's one rainy morning. The roads were wet and the pole and platform of our open back LD were pretty slippery by then. I was inside as we left the last stop at the bottom of Hamlet Court Rd, to start crossing over the railway line at Westcliff Station, when there was a huge commotion on the platform. I turned to see a hand sliding down the pole and a jaw hitting the platform with what I thought was a quite a thud, before disappearing from view. By the time I had given four bells (emergency stop) and we had come to a stop, the man in question was nowhere to be seen! Fortunately there were two women seated on the bench seats beside the platform and also a pedestrian came forward, who were prepared to provide details as witnesses.

Apparently the man had made a running leap to board the moving bus, and misjudged the distance. Although he managed to grab the pole, his foot slipped off the platform and we must have dragged him a short way before he finally let go. Why he disappeared before we could stop and make sure he was alright is still beyond me. I can only assume he was fearful of getting into some kind of trouble. The pedestrian said he had rolled onto his feet, got up and started running away, in the opposite direction from which we were travelling: back up Hamlet Court Rd, before turning into a side street! He was nowhere to be seen by the time I was able to get off and look. Needless to say that lunch time was spent filling in a report just to make sure we were covered.

Winter

The weather played a role in another accident too. This time Johnny was skillfully, cautiously and uneventfully negotiating an overnight snowfall on our way to Lower Hockley one February morning. That is until we got to Rawreth Lane, when I happened to notice a Ford Anglia gracefully gliding along the road, with all four wheels locked. It caught us square, amidships, between the platform doors and rear wheels. Names and numbers, and some good-natured laughs were exchanged before we went on our way without further incident, except for the paperwork when we got back to the depot. Needless to say, Coventry Hill (Hullbridge), Crown Hill (Rayleigh), Eastwood Rise and the hill up to Prittlewell Church were all pretty sporty that morning!

Later that winter we had to contend with a flood at the end of the Hullbridge Road and the then, aptly named, Watery Lane. The water managed to reach up to the platform doors, but did not flow through the downstairs as it had done on some previous occasions. There were several stories of FLF's going through with the platform doors open at the front, the emergency door open at the back, and a river running through between the two!

The Nasty Old Man from Leigh

It was a hot and humid summer's lunchtime during my second summer and I was running a circuit of short 25's. An old fellow boarded at Leigh Church and went upstairs and sat on the nearside. "Just going round the corner mate" he said, and paid the minimum fare with his OAP pass. He was still on after we had got to Leigh Hotel.

"How far you going?" "Next stop mate!"

I rang the bell. A few people boarded but still he didn't get off. Soon we had reached Chalkwell Park Schools. Enough was enough!

"I'm not going to take you all the way to Southend! Either pay up or get off now!" "What you gonna do, pick me up and throw me off. I can still take you anytime, Sonny."

I still had a good number of other perfectly reasonable fare-paying passengers on board, expecting to continue their journeys onto Westcliff or Southend. It was then that fate presented me with the first of two strokes of good luck. An SD-crewed Canvey pulled up behind. I hastily arranged a transfer of my other passengers, hurriedly completing the necessary paperwork to do so. So now it was just me, my driver Tom and the nasty, belligerent old man from Leigh upstairs.

"We're not going to move until you either pay up of get off!"

"I'm not in a hurry. Besides you'll still have to throw me off". And so it went on, until that second stroke of good luck. Being upstairs on the near side, my nasty recalcitrant old passenger did not have a good view of everything around him. So he was oblivious to my driver Tom flagging down a passing Panda Car, until he was trapped upstairs by one of Southend's finest on the platform:

"'Allo 'Allo 'Allo what's going on 'ere then?" Well, actually he didn't say that, but when he got upstairs, he did recognize the old man in question – "Oh! It's you," and he duly escorted the now succumbed and very obedient passenger off the bus. I thought little more of it, apart from the paperwork that still needed to be completed, and the whole thing gradually receded into the evening, as surely did the day. Until I got home that is: "So what was all the fuss with the Police?" enquired my brother who had apparently driven past at the precisely the moment Tom and I were explaining to the Constable what was going on!

Miscellaneous Memories

However, it wasn't just the problem journeys that stick in mind. There were always other memorable events…

First Hullbridge and the Police Chase

That was not my only incident with the Police! On another occasion we were running the first Hullbridge. This duty began at 4.41 AM and involved taking out the FLF that was parked up in the bus wash overnight. For me, it meant either my Dad would get up and drive me in, or I'd ride my bike the 10 or so miles into Southend, via Ashingdon and Rochford, to take the bus back to where I'd just come from! Surprisingly, there were a couple of regulars who relied on that outbound. On the return there was little more to do after the first few commuters had got to Rayleigh Station, except a few early birds starting making their way to Progress Road or into Southend from Kent Elms onwards. We had just descended down Eastwood Rise and were approaching Progress Road, when I became very aware that a police car was, basically, "chasing" us. This was not difficult to do as we were progressing only at a stately 20–25 mph!

We stopped at Progress Road to wait up a bit, and sure enough so does the Police car and out gets the Bobby, definitely not in Sweeney-style, and approaches the doors: Johnny opens them.

"Have you just come from Hullbridge?"

"Er …yes?" I replied, hesitantly. He continued, and this is the God's-honest truth – "Well I was wondering if you saw an advert for an aquarium that's for sale in the newsagent's window while you were down there?"

"No?

"Oh OK then." He got back into his car and off he went!

Johnny meanwhile is looking at me very perplexed through the bulkhead window, so I get out and lean across the bonnet to tell him.

"What the @#$% ?!" he says, slides his window shut and off we go too!

Nasty Fumes and the VR

One complaint that would often require a change of vehicle was the smell of diesel coming into the passenger compartment. Whilst it didn't happen that often, when it did happen, it was, well, pretty obnoxious; the only recourse was to call in and request for a replacement vehicle to be waiting for you at SCB, or similar.

So one evening early in my second summer (1975), as Johnny and I were about to make our way down to pick up a 22 to Hullbridge, we were called downstairs and told that the crew bringing the bus into Southend, from Shoebury, had complained of diesel fumes, and we needed to take a new bus along with us.

"Which one should we take?" asked Johnny, knowing that by this time of the evening pretty much any bus that was in the garage would be OK to take, including possibly a Semi (-automatic FLF), normally reserved for Wood Green or Grays'.

"Any one you want".

OK, that one!" said Johnny "Yeah, that one!!" I added.

We were both pointing to a VR that was parked up against the wall.

"Sure" said Derek, who was in charge of vehicle allocations at the time. "Really?"

"Yeah, go on!"

We swiftly took that VR out of the garage before anyone had chance to change their mind! I'm pretty certain that it was the first time a crewed VR had operated a 22, and it could be that it was also the last! I even suggested to Johnny that he take my ticket machine and give me the rest of the night off! However, our jaunt was relatively short lived. As we turned into SCB on the return to Shoebury, there was Derek on the 22 stand with another FLF.

"Hope you boys had a nice trip!" he smiled.

FLF's and the Boiling Radiator

The other common mechanical problem, especially on the FLF's with the Cave-Brown-Cave "cooling" system, was boiling over. Although these were generally not dealt with by replacing the vehicle, but by adding water! There were always places to get this from, including the ubiquitous end-of-route cafes. Other places were a little less convenient though. Gants Hill and Newbury Park seemed to be favourite spots for a boil over, which meant just waiting up for a bit. Most of the time these were temporary conditions because of heavy traffic, but if they were persistent, it would result in a call to Brentwood garage, hopefully for some watery relief at the High Street . My first mate, Bill, would ascribe this equipment failure to a "*@!$%^&* useless idea," much to the (no doubt unfelt) chagrin of Messrs. Cave, Brown and Cave!

Steve and the Long 3

Now it wasn't often that you don't even manage to complete a trip! But I managed it with Steve. He was a conductor buddy of mine, who finally took the plunge and completed his driver training. It was a Saturday afternoon underneath an overcast grey sky that was threatening rain. But we were in good sprits: it was Steve's first 3 as a driver, and it was at the end of a good day's overtime for me. We picked up a pretty well loaded 3, and the London Road was pretty heavy going. Steve was a little tentative and I could see we were starting to fall behind schedule by Leigh Elms. Of course the later we got, the more passengers we picked up and so we got even slower. By the time we got to Benfleet we were well behind. And we finally arrived at Leigh Beck a good 20 minutes or more behind schedule.

There was not time for a break, we turned around immediately and headed back. By the time we got back to the London Rd, we were behind other buses we should have been in front of, which actually cut us a bit of a break, until we got to SD. The trip out of Vic Circus was very heavy going, and Steve was feeling the pressure of being so far behind schedule. In fact, by the time we had reached Thorpe Bay Station, the 3 behind had caught up with us. A hastily thought up excuse of a "slow bus" convinced our remaining passengers that they would be better off completing their journeys on the bus behind, which was no doubt true. So we quickly transferred passengers and went down to Maplin Way to turn around, no doubt to the surprise of the locals in the neighbourhood. We simply resumed our return at Thorpe Bay Station and managed to only be a few minutes late getting back to SD! We handed over to the next crew with a "busy coming out of Shoebury" comment, and nobody was any the wiser (I think)? I took Steve upstairs for much-needed, therapeutic 'weak and sweet,' although I think he needed something much, much stronger!

Pea-Souper and the Late 3

On another occasion the fog had become very thick as we left Leigh Beck for the last 3 back from Canvey: a veritable 'pea-souper!' Visibility was very restricted which made it slow going across the Island and through Benfleet. I figured it would be a lot clearer once we'd topped Bread & Cheese Hill in Thundersley. I was wrong. In fact it seemed like it was getting worse as we got closer to Southend. Passenger and road traffic was, needless to say, pretty light: mostly the last few stragglers after closing time. What few cars there were, however, seemed to be reluctant to pass us on the few occasions we did stop. By the time we had dropped our last passenger at the Cricketers in Westcliff, we had quite the procession behind us. I signalled to Johnny that we were empty. So when we got to the roundabout before Vic Circus, by the SCT depot, instead of continuing on down, Johnny swung round and took the short cut back to the Depot, down the Old London Rd, past the bus wash. And, lo and behold, so did half the cars that were following us, I guess thinking that we were still going into the centre of town! I can just imagine their surprise as we swung into the depot, and they found out they'd gone down a dead-end!

Sea Fronts and the Pier

These were always my favourite diversion. Apart from a few folks going from the White Horse to Temple Sutton, or from Leigh back to Kent Elms, most of the people who were on a Seafront, actually wanted to be on the bus! There was something very relaxing about proceeding in a deliberate, stately and unhurried fashion along the Prom – after all, a 20-something year old KSW was not likely to do much else! – in the open air with the unmistakable taste of the salt in the breeze. As I said before, it took me along some unfamiliar territory given the OMO workings of the time, but the highlight was always going under the Pier.

Given the limited clearance everybody had to be sitting down upstairs before the bus could proceed under it. This involved stopping the bus, standing on the stairs, warning all passengers to remain seated, and then ringing the bell so the bus could proceed slowly under. Inevitably someone would reach up and try to touch the underneath, and those that succeeded received a nasty sting for their troubles. But I never had an incident of some fool trying to see how close he or she could get their head to it without actually being hit – although once or twice some did look like they were going to try! A gruffly barked "Sit down" usually did the trick, but my hand was always poised, ready to hit four bells if needed.

Strikers and the Poker Game

Being unionized (part of the TGWU), there was always the possibility of some industrial action, which would not have helped me much, since my goal was to work lots and save money! So I was quite fortunate to only have one to deal with. Jack McArdle, a conductor, was our union rep in Southend, and it was one afternoon when everybody was called out. I can't even remember what the reason was. Alan, one of the drivers, lived nearby, so a group of us went there and played poker all afternoon. I actually earned more there than I would have working half my regular shift! The whole thing was over by the evening, and I went back to finish whatever was left of my shift.

We were also indirectly affected by other strikes too. There were a couple of occasions when there were London Transport strikes, which meant we couldn't operate in the LT area and complete a full Wood Green. When this happened we ran through to Brentwood and turned around there, after obligatory cup of tea at BD. I'm not sure what happened with the 2's to Grays at those times, but I'm pretty certain we couldn't run all the way through as Grays was definitely LT territory. I can only assume they turned at Stanford-le-Hope, or Orsett. But they made for an interesting diversion, and a chance to do something a little different from normal.

Squaddies and the Skinheads

For two or three days there had been some sort of running skirmish between some of the Squaddies and a bunch of skinheads around the Shoebury barracks and beach areas. So we were warned to watch for any potential trouble particularly on the 3's and 5's. Although we didn't experience any trouble, we did see a couple of lads disappear through a door in a wall as we were on our way on a 5 from Blackgate Road. In close pursuit was a huge (and I mean huge!) Regimental Sergeant Major. He appeared to just lean back and kick the door down, and as he followed them through. I hope for their sakes he never actually managed to catch up to them!!

Christmas Eve and the Decorated Bus

Working around the holidays was a bind, but getting the last Wood Green on Christmas Eve – well I guess as the new kid, I drew the short straw! I was scheduled to go with Tim, one of the other younger crew drivers, although I can't remember why he wasn't doing this with his regular mate, Steve. Anyway in a flash of inspiration we decided it would be fun to decorate the bus for Christmas. So Steve and I quickly ran down Southend High St to get whatever balloons, streamers, tinsel and other decorations we could find, and met Tim at SCB. It was there that Steve decided he would come with us! The journey up was pretty sedate, mostly with folks on their way out for the evening. Steve and I were planning where we were going to put all the decorations we had bought. As soon as we got to WG, the three of us set about decorating the bus, having blown up the balloons on the way in, from around Walthamstow onwards.

Coming back was a blast. Everybody thought the idea was just the ticket (pun intended!) Everyone got on and off with "Merry Christmas" or similar, although there were no kisses under the mistletoe! Most of the balloons had burst, or been popped by the time we reached Rayleigh, but the all the other decorations held fast pretty much. So when my Dad picked me up and drove me home and I was ready to enjoy Christmas.

Gants Hill and the Slash

It was a bright sunny summer Sunday and Johnny and I were scheduled to work a spare – just turn up and wait and see who doesn't! The day was promising to be a real scorcher! It seemed to us that pretty much everyone had turned up for work, despite the promise of the glorious day that was unfolding, when we were called down from the canteen: "Driver Corder,

Conductor Harper we have a job for you." Apparently, it had been reported that there were some pretty significant crowds waiting to get down to Southend for the day. "We want you to run up to Gants Hill (Ilford), and come back a few minutes ahead of schedule in front of the regular 251." Our very own Slash! They found us a spare semi (-automatic Lodekka) and off we went. We confused the crew working the 151 to Canvey somewhat, when they rounded Gants Hill to find us waiting there, still marked Private. But as soon as they left, I changed the blinds to Southend/251 and we waited. By the time we left, about five minutes ahead of normal, we had quite a few passengers – and a good two-thirds load by the time we reach Romford (still keeping just a couple of minutes ahead of normal schedule). I had to show my waybill to a Lurker we picked up in Harold Hill, to prove we weren't the normal service running early. He got out at Brentwood (time for a cuppa I suppose!), and then we picked up the pace a little figuring that we had got the "London crowd" we were meant to! It was a much better way to spend the day than just sitting in the depot. By the time we got back, we were well into the shift and were told we could go home: A fine day's work: a Slash and a short shift!

The Old Man and the Old RT

It was at Mawney's roundabout in Romford that he boarded. I'd say he was in his seventies, and he was on his way to Turnpike Lane. During the quieter moments, especially in the London half of a Wood Green, I'd often take off my trusty Setright and lodge it in the handrail underneath the bulkhead window downstairs, and stand (or sit) there looking forward. He sat in the very first seat on the left, right by the doors.

"It's not like the old RT"

I turned round. "'beg pardon?"

"It's not like the old RT. This – it's not like the old RT" "I'm sorry, what old RT?"

"I used to like the old RT. They don't run 'em anymore you know. They used to. Used to get 'em all the time. It's not like the old RT, this!"

And so it continued, any time I was within earshot: Newbury Park, Redbridge, Walthamstow, Tottenham Hale…… At last Turnpike Lane, he got up to get off:

Thanks. Lovely journey mate. But, it's not like the old RT!"

Ironically, for him to travel to Turnpike Lane from Romford on a 251, it could never have been "like the old RT:" EN, like Westcliff or City before hand, wouldn't have operated RT's! At least, not the kind LT operated. So I can only suspect he may be equating the "old RT" with some of 'deckers that City Coach/Westcliff might have run in days gone by.

Kent Elms Corner and the Guide Dog

Well the stop before actually. Since we did work a variety of routes at a variety of times no two days were alike. And, although you might recognize the same faces on occasions, I found that there were few "regulars" that stood out from the crowd, apart from the few that would be on a first Hullbridge or Canvey and the like. However, there was one particular gentleman who was blind. I actually can't remember now quite where he would get on, but he always got off at the stop before Kent Elms Corner, coming out of Southend. Funnily enough, I don't really remember him ever getting on at the stop after Kent Elms on the way in! But I do remember that his dog would always start moving him towards the door, before we had reached the stop. It has always fascinated me how the dog knew when to get up. After all, he was always under the seat and not looking out of the window at any visual clues. Furthermore, every trip would be different vis-à-vis the time, number of stops and so on. If I was upstairs I would always come down in time, to make sure that he would get off at his stop. But inevitably, the dog had beaten me to it. I'm convinced the dog must have got up and rung the bell on some occasions!

Overtime and lots of it

Given that I was saving money for college, I sought overtime as often as I could, especially on those days where it paid well: namely scheduled weekend days off. So I was delighted when the opportunity to work some early overtime on a Saturday (good pay) came up and I took the second Wood Green out in the morning. I'd be back in time for lunch, and even maybe squeeze in a couple 25's or 29's or maybe a round of 6's before going home. The trip up to the smoke was uneventful and when I got back, sure enough there was more overtime available for me to do. "It's a little long," the Inspector said, but I didn't mind: I had nothing planned for the day anyway, and Sunday off too! So off I went – to Grays! But I was still in good spirits when I got back, there was still some daylight left: "Conductor Harper, can you come to the office?" They asked me if I'd like to just a little more: "Just one run." I should have known better, but the greed gland was throbbing and, of course, I said yes, without enquiring after the details – maybe a quick trip to Sutton Cemetery, or Newington Ave. "Sure" I heard myself say without really thinking, and accepting the duty card. I unrolled it: "Grays – again?!" "Think of the overtime," said the Inspector working the office that day, smiling wryly. He was right: it would be nearly half a-weeks wages for one, albeit long day's work. By the end of it I was ready for my bed, and grateful for the Sunday off too. But, it was one of those "red letter" days: not the ultimate, fabled two Wood Greens and a Grays but a real close second – a Wood Green and two Grays!

Wimbledon and the 251

OK the 251's went to Wood Green, not Wimbledon: but it was the Men's final, and Connors' was favoured to win. I liked watching Jimmy Connors play so it was a little disappointing to have to leave Southend to go to Wood Green, just as he was getting going with all his grunts and strains. Try as I may, asking anyone who looked like they might know how he was doing as they got on, I had no luck. As we turned into the depot, I literally flew off the bus and up to the canteen to hopefully see the final moments as Connors triumphed with Championship point to secure the Wimbledon

Men's title and lift that glorious cup. But it was over. "Who won?" I asked the other crew there. Arthur Ashe had just won his historic victory!

Fortunately, not every day had such stories to tell, but those that did are still vividly seared into my memory like they were yesterday! Most, however, were just ordinary. But, looking back, I have come to realize how profound this brief experience was for me. One that I am extremely lucky to have had, and wouldn't have traded for anything else.

I have tried to describe, albeit probably inadequately, what it was like for a young lad to fulfill a boy hood ambition to work on the buses, and capture the essence of what that job entailed. It wasn't just "ringing bells and taking fares." It was more a way of life that seeps into your blood! I still hanker for it, even today, as you will no doubt gather in this conclusion..

Return to the Glory Days

In his excellent book on the Glory Days of Eastern National (EN), Richard Delahoy makes the statement that in his "biased" opinion, the 31 ft long semi-automatic version of the FLF was "among the finest buses ever built" (e.g. http://www.sct61.org.uk/gallery/engall5/en2614). I would like to shed further light on that comment, from my perspective. In addition to my experience of actually working on the various Bristol 'deckers (K, LD/FS, FLF and VR), I have also had the pleasure of travelling on many other different models over the years: Regent III/RT, Regent V, Routemaster, Bridgemaster, Renown, Guy Arab IV, Leyland PD2, 3, Lowlander, and a Loline in the time I spent at Southampton, with trips to Leeds, Leicester, Reading, Nottingham, Cardiff and so on, as well as those since moving to the U.S. Consequently, I think Richard's point can be unequivocally put to rest with the following story.

Johnny and I were working the first Wood Green of the day, which for me meant getting up very early to ride my bike the 10 miles from Hullbridge to SD, as was often the case on these early starts (or the reverse on late finishes). Despite the morning chill, the sunrise beckoned a fine day and the prospect of some good overtime! It was the usual rush hour crawl by the time we got up into "the smoke," but nothing out of the ordinary otherwise. The morning return would be equally uneventful, except perhaps for the ongoing road works around South Woodford and Redbridge.

As we got set to depart Wood Green, there was smallish suitcase placed in the luggage pen inside, and an elderly lady had occupied one of the single seats beside the stair-well, up top. I was always struck how the terms "up top" and "inside" had prevailed: a throwback to the days when all double deckers were open on top of the lower (covered) saloon. Throughout the journey we exchanged pleasantries several times: she was on her way to see her sister in Southend for a few weeks and was looking forward to their "strolls along the sea front." She particularly enjoyed travelling through the "countryside" between Shenfield and Wickford.

By the time we turned into Southend Central Bus Station the sun was gleaming brightly over the estuary, silhouetting the Pier. I set her suitcase outside on the pavement. As she picked it up, she leant into me and beamed "Thank you for such a pleasant journey – just like it used to be!" "An', he's very good for a youngster," she added pointing at the cab. "'Ave yourselves a nice cuppa!" and handed me a 50p tip!

She was right. I couldn't help feeling just a little tinge of pride to be wearing my EN dust jacket that morning, as we pulled out to return to SD. We had upheld a long tradition of quality, reliable service first started by City Coaches, by providing an excellent, smooth journey fashioned out of couple of key ingredients: I was indeed crewing with a very good driver and he was behind the wheel of undoubtedly the finest British half-cab 'decker ever built, bar none (with due respect and apologies to all those other fine vehicles, but I'm sorry – not really even close)!

This point was further underscored many years later, in New York in 1998. For several years I worked for a company that provided vehicle maintenance software to transit operators in the U.S.A. On one of my many visits to New York City Transit I had the opportunity to participate in a demonstration ride of one of their newly sanctioned buses. Our host spent the hour or so ride from and to their Central Maintenance facility in Brooklyn, extolling the virtues of the 'new' technology which now made Low Floor/Flat Floor vehicles possible. The man seemed utterly incredulous when I mentioned to him, privately, that this had been possible since the Fifties in the UK! Furthermore the ride wasn't the best as the bus had a pretty harsh fully automatic gear box, which seemed to lurch from one gear to another as it changed. It certainly didn't have the smoothness of the driver-shifted semi automatic gear box I had become accustomed to those many years earlier. So much for thirty-plus years of progress!

Favourites

Sadly, a few short weeks after that run to WG, Johnny and I made our final run together on a 27 to Canvey. I had worked from the start of one summer (1974) to the end of the next (1975). A lot of experience had been packed into just 15 months. When we got back to SD, I bagged up my money, handed in my Setright and uniform, shook Johnny by the hand, gave Joyce a hug goodbye and left to go to the University of Southampton.

On balance my favourite duty was the long Wood Green, even those that had a few shorts tacked on the end, for example a round of 61's or 29's. Conversely, if I had to choose my least favourite, it was the 5 from Shoebury's Blackgate Rd to Canvey Leigh Beck. I was never quite sure where I was when we turned right off the London Road at the bottom of Bread and Cheese Hill, up Kents Hill Rd North and again when we went through the Newlands section on Canvey. In fact there was one fare stage that I never actually managed to work out where it was! For the shorter routes in town, I loved doing the 6/A's the best, but never really liked the 29A's. Of course the 67's along the Seafront were always a fun diversion, and the 22's were always nice, since I lived in Hullbridge, they were very familiar. Like home!

The Following Summer

In 1976 I managed to wangle my way back for a third summer to get a couple more months under my belt. As far as I could make out SD only hired three conductors for that summer, including me. On my first run, I took over a 6 from Joyce. There lots of hugs and smiles and welcome backs and cups of tea (later) in the canteen. It was good to see many of the old gang again: Joyce, Steve, Phil, Ray, The Winters, Tim, Alan, Eric and Rene, and of course Johnny.

Even 'he' was a joy to listen to as 'he' recounted some Australian tale or another, well – for the first time at any rate! Trevor, however, said it was that I just couldn't keep away from him!

But things had changed. The first significant change when I returned that following summer (1976) was that there were no more open-backers, apart from the Seafronts. All the LD's and the FS had gone. I don't recall too much of a cut back in the crew duties at SD by that point. While there were no more 14's, and short relief's on 3's and 7's, the extra FLF's needed must have been allocated in from the more rural parts of the fleet, where the move to One-Man-Operation (OMO) would have been much more significant. It had always been fun, when working 6's, short 25's, 29's or 61's to be able to lean off the back of the platform onto the bonnet of the bus behind and have quick chat with that driver, at Victoria Circus for instance. But, alas, those days were gone.

I also don't recall any "three bell-ers," either, rung when the bus was fully loaded to avoid picking anyone else up. Even the commuter runs to and from Rayleigh, Benfleet and Thorpe Bay stations didn't seem quite as frantic anymore. Yet despite the inevitable decline in passengers, making the progress to even more OMO services inevitable, it was often easy to find yourself running behind schedule because of traffic congestion. Saturday afternoons in Southend were particularly challenging, where trying to make it through the town centre in the allotted time had become next to impossible.

Crew shortages were also becoming an issue, making the move to OMO even more needed. On a few occasions we would handover to a

Corporation OMO, instead of an EN crew. But, crewing behind a variety of drivers for those several weeks, including several more runs with Johnny working overtime, I still managed to enjoy earning a little more towards my college kitty.

Perhaps the most memorable was when Dave, another Conductor, and I were both working 67's one weekday afternoon and had a running 'skirmish' each time we passed one another along the seafront! It started with a few crumpled up coin bags hurled from one open top deck to another, but escalated to the launching of "opened" ticket rolls, which unfurled as they sailed through the air!

However, sadly, that September, I finally hung up my trusty old Setright for good! It wasn't quite as wrenching this time as I hadn't been paired up with a regular driver, but I knew I wouldn't be coming back for several reasons. Firstly, there wouldn't be an opportunity to do so because of a big summer project for my degree the following year, and secondly I seriously doubted there would be a job to come back to! Ironically my last duty was Shoebury/5 followed by an early-evening Hullbridge. For the former, I was determined to find that one mysterious fare stage I had never previously found – but I completely missed it (again)! So that evening, after cashing out for the very last time and saying good-bye to whoever was left in canteen, which by then were very few, it was a slow melancholy walk across from SD to Vic Circus get the following 22 home. The conductor recognized me and gave me one last 'free' crew ride home as a parting gift. The only things I took away with me were my enamel EN badge, a last glimpse of a dimly lit SD depot disappearing into the evening's fading gloom, and a lifetime of experiences, packed into, as it turns out, only actually 19 total months of working on the buses! But what a blast!!

Close Encounters of the Recent Kind

For the past twenty four years or so now I have been living in the United States. Yet even here, I have managed to stumble across the occasional Lodekka, in my travels. The first was on a trip to Boston, where the company had hired an open top bus to take us from a downtown hotel to the harbour for dinner at a conference one evening. To my absolute pleasure it was an FLF. Despite much garish paint inside and out, and good deal of conversion with the passenger doors now being on the right, instead of the left, there were still some vestiges of Tilling green to be seen. Unfortunately there was not enough detail left to identify its original owner. I have also seen a shorter front entrance Lodekka (FSF) used as a mobile chip shop at the Highland games held in Pleasanton, California; another FSF was "on duty" as a booking office for Gray Line tours in San Francisco; and an FLF used as factory storage shed near San Jose airport.

Most recently I happened across two of them being used as a video games "room" and a smoking "room" adjacent to the British-themed Cameron's Pub in Half Moon Bay, California. As is customary in the U.S. these are falsely painted an LT-type bright red, and probably by now consists of parts of several vehicles. One of two (left, with the somewhat disinterested family) has the very faintest of traces of its rear vehicle registration left. As best as I can make out, it starts with what looks like 'something-OO', which would make it a 1962 EN vehicle, or at least that's where that part of it came from!

Also, in a second-hand bookshop in San Ramon, California, where I now live, I also stumbled across a book called "Buses & Coaches 1945–1965." As I was thumbing through it, something caught my eye. It was, oddly enough, a chimney stack! But a very recognisable one: sure enough it was the Anchor Inn at Hullbridge, with an ex-Westcliff K5G ready to depart on a service 22 to Leigh Rectory Hotel. Upon further inspection, the book also contained 2600, one of the magnificent CH37/18F "X10" FLF coaches at Victoria and 4200, a DP41F LS on Coach-Air service at Euston Square en–route to Southend Airport. Naturally I had to buy the book!

But, perhaps the most evocative encounter was one summer's morning on one of my many trips to New York. I was walking from my hotel on my way to a meeting at Park Ave and 55th St, when a memory was stirred, awakened deep within my mind: echoing around the cavernous corporate canyons of mid-town Manhattan was the unmistakable "song" of a very familiar "bird.**" It was a Gardner 6 cylinder engine being put through its paces in the lower ratios of a 'crash' gear box. I hurried quickly to next intersection to see the rear of an open-top FLF on sightseeing duty, disappearing cross-town. Amid my revelry, I was carried far away from the sultry morning heat of New York City on the tail of that sound, to, maybe, Victoria Circus, or was it somewhere along the Eastwood Road from Rayleigh?

"Where to luv?..."

"One and a half to Kent Elms?" "That'll be 12p"

"Much obliged... Any more fares please?..."

MH

MH would have passed and called at Southend Victoria Station during his time with ENOC; this picture shows a collection of ENOC buses in the forecourt of the then named Southend Station in 1947. The nearest to the camera is an unidentified Bristol L awaiting departure on Service 19A which would take 3 hours and 23 minutes to reach Clacton-on –Sea. The LNER train journey would not be short either at around 2 hours and 40 minutes, because of changes required at Shenfield and Chelmsford. This would be the last year before the creation of British Railways in 1948 and the LNER (London and North Eastern Railway) sign can be seen showing Southend, the station would subsequently be known as Southend Victoria from 1st May, 1949.

Tales from the Cab and the Platform

I was a bus driver for Eastern National during the Conductor era:

Two bells to start the bus;

One ring to stop at the next stop;

Three rings, bus full, don't stop to pick up passengers until you get the stop signal;

Four bells or more, emergency, cut out the engine, hand brake on and run round to the platform to find the conductor and sort out problem, which could be an ill passenger or a stroppy one who did not want to pay his fare. In any event, we do not move until the problem is sorted.

My first day as a driver at Brentwood was the 262 town service which ran to and from the Bishops Hall Estate in the north to the East Ham Estate (Hornbeam Close) to the south. We took the bus over a short walk from the depot at the North Road lay-by in Ongar Road, which has a pub and various shops including a pet shop. My conductor for that day was a grumpy old sod and a proper company man. I got in the cab, started up, but did not get two bells to go. Then I looked in the nearside mirror and noticed the conductor coming to the cab. "Have you got my transfer waybill?" he asked. Now this is a piece of paper which a conductor leaves for the next one when handing over part way through a journey. Obviously as it was my first day I did not know what a waybill was, so I thought for a moment and decided it must be some type of tropical bird he had lost, like a parrot. So I suggested he call in the pet shop to see if anyone had handed it in. "Are you being ****ing funny", he said. He was a grumpy old sod for the rest of the day and told the manager he did not want to work with me again!

My regular conductor Jim was very different. He had three pleasures in life: women, horse racing and beer – in that order! Our favourite route was the 40, Chelmsford to Tilbury Ferry via Brentwood and Ockendon. We often changed shifts with other crews to get on that route. One day during the summer we had a very bad storm which made us run late. As I had a

Leyland decker which was much faster than the old Bristol's, I decided to push it to make up time. After leaving Widford on the dual carriageway A12, I noticed a motorcyclist trying to overtake, so I decided to give him a burn up (ie, a race). We were neck and neck until we came to a hill and then he went past after I thought I had given him a good soaking. Then as he passed I noticed he had a pillion passenger. I thought to myself, that looks like my conductor on the back of that motorbike. Then he stuck two fingers up. It was my conductor!! What the hell is he doing on the back of a motorbike when he is supposed to be on the back of this bus? As he went into the distance I pulled into the next lay-by and got out to tell my passengers that I was now without a conductor.

One lady passenger said "I saw your conductor, driver, on the back of a motorbike and he stuck two fingers up to you. Your conductor is a very rude man". "Quite, madam. Now as I have no conductor, I may have to terminate this bus at Brentwood. I will drive to the Spread Eagle pub where there is a phone box and contact the bus company". I got back in the cab and carried on to the Spread Eagle, where among the passengers waiting was a very wet and dirty conductor! He was very angry and called me some obscene names and said that I had thrown him off the bus. I said I never did, I have been sitting in the cab all the time. He then explained that when I went round Widford roundabout very fast on two wheels he was thrown off. The bloke on motorbike was following the bus, saw what happened and gave him a pillion ride.

I got out of the cab and went with him to the platform. In his cubby hole where the waybill was kept, I noticed his racing paper was missing so I asked him where it was. "On the Widford Roundabout", he said. I replied "So that's it, you were not holding on 'very tight please' like you tell your passengers to, you had your head in that paper". He did not reply, but as he went round the bus to collect the fares he told the passengers, "I hope you all have your life insurance paid up, as we have a madman driving this bus". Then my lady passenger piped up "I saw you on the back of a motor bike and you stuck two fingers up to your driver. You are a very rude man, conductor". Of course, I agreed with her! So Jim told me to get back in that cab. I said "Alright darling" to him; "Don't darling me" he replied. So I put my arms round him and gave him a peck on the cheek and said "darling, promise me you will never leave me again like that".

That did it! He picked up a passenger's umbrella with a spike on, hit me across the head with it and then put the point somewhere in my anatomy it was never intended to go! He chased me off the bus and pointing with the umbrella said "Get in that ***ing cab!" By now I was in danger of dying through laughing, I had to hold on to the head lights to stop myself falling on the floor. He then rang the bell like a fire alarm. I got in the cab and drove off still laughing. He kept hitting the destination box with a coin and jumping on the floor above my head, which made me laugh even more. By now Jim had become the greatest showman and I could hear passengers laughing at his antics. At Brentwood many passengers came up to my cab and said we should be on TV as we were better than Blakey or Butler from On The Buses.

We were nearly 30 minutes down (late) and from now on speeding would not be enough to make up time, we needed low flying! I looked round to see where Jim was as I didn't want to lose him for a second time. He was sitting down in the saloon reading a newspaper – the crafty so-and-so had scrounged it from one of the passengers and was at the racing pages again. After having my foot in the bucket until we got to South Ockendon, I noticed the 370 (London Transport) ahead of us. Now he went the same route as us, so he would be picking up any passengers for Grays and Tilbury, and this gave me an idea. I stopped at the next bus stop and flashed the saloon lights to get Jim to come round to the front. I told him to find out if we had any punters on for Grays and to find out where they want to get off. One wanted Cuckoo Corner, the rest the Tilbury Ferry terminus. So after dropping off at Cuckoo Corner, it was saloon lights off, head down the A13 to Daneholes roundabout at Socketts Heath, then through Chadwell St Mary to pick up our route again at Tilbury Iron Bridge, missing out Grays completely! We arrived at the Ferry 5 minutes early, so Jim was delighted. This meant we could get a couple of pints in at the Railway Club on the station before going back – we were scheduled a 15 minute layover there. As we were leaving, the 370 was just coming in. The driver said "Where did you pass me, I never saw you?" I said that we overfly!!

We had a steady run back but we were aware that due to strict licencing hours, all the pubs would be shut when we got to Brentwood. So when we got to the Thatcher's Arms at Warley at 10.10 pm, Jim advised our passengers that we would have a 20 minute refreshment break there. So it was lights out again, while we all adjourned to the pub. One of our lady passengers said she thought it was very kind of us to think of the passengers like this and said we must be the most efficient crew on Eastern National. "We are madam, without a shadow of doubt" Jim replied!

Jim, my conductor, missed the bus twice more after our Widford roundabout incident. On one trip we arrived at the Brentwood terminus and while passengers were alighting, I decided to use the toilets close by. Jim, whose three pastimes were women, horse racing and beer, as you'll recall from page 124, also decided that as the betting shop was by the bus stop, it would be a good idea to have a little flutter. The problem with Jim was that when he entered a betting shop, he was on another planet and instead of being a conductor, he became a jockey.

I came back to the bus and assumed he was on board, so I drove off on our dead run to our next starting point, about 5 miles away at the shirt factory at North Ockendon. When I got there I found I was talking to myself – then I thought "betting shop"! I decided that as my passengers would be weekly ticket holders going home, I would not need a conductor until I got to Brentwood Station, where I could pick Jim up again. So I explained this to my passengers and away we went. All was going well until I got to the waterworks at Great Warley, where I picked up a "jumper" – Inspector Ernie. He gave me a nice smile and a wave and gave the starting signal when he got on. But I did not move – I waited until panic set in. This took all of about 6 seconds, when I got five bells – emergency stop! He came running to the cab and said "Where is your conductor?". Me: "At Brentwood Station". Inspector: "What's he doing there?" Me: "Well, it took him longer to get a bet on than it did for me to have a pee. I have his ticket machine and box here in the cab so if you want to get busy, get the fares in". He then said "I don't have much choice, do I." He was *not* happy!

At the station, Jim was waiting. He came up to my cab so I said "don't make excuses, you are redundant, I have Inspector Ernie collecting the fares". Jim's face took on the scream mask! The outcome was that we both got a disciplinary letter, Jim for abandoning the bus and me for driving off without the starting signal and operating the bus without a conductor. But we got off, as I said if it was not for Inspector Ernie reporting us, no one would have known any thing about it.

The next time Jim missed the bus was at Blackmore. I left him in the lower deck while I got in the cab and drove off. At the first stop about 2 miles up the road, I did not get the starting signal so I went round the back and found him missing. I asked my passengers if he was on the bus when they had got on. They said he was not. I thought he must still be at Blackmore, but there are no betting shops there. I thought I would have to go back for him and was wondering where I was going to turn the bus round, when a police car pulled up behind the bus with blue lights flashing. I wondered if I'd run him over. The police driver beckoned me over and asked "Do you recognize this man in the back, sir?". It was Jim. Without dropping my guard, I said "No officer, I can honestly say I have never seen that man before in my life. Who is he?". They thought it very funny. Then I shouted at Jim "What the hell are you doing in the back of a police car when you are supposed to be on the back of this bus!".

When Jim got out of the police car, he explained that after I'd got into the cab, he had got his racing paper from under the stairs but dropped it and it fell into the road. He thought he had time to retrieve it before I moved off, but I was too quick for him and he could not catch me. He was just about to go into the pub until I came back for him, when he saw the police car and stopped it to ask for a lift!

When the new deckers (FLF Lodekkas) with doors came in, I was able to contain Jim a lot better. Every time I left the bus with Jim inside I closed the doors. He could get out by pressing the emergency button, but he could not close them again. So if I came back and found the doors open, I knew Jim had escaped again and it was time to look in the nearest betting shop or pub for a bus conductor – or, as I called him, my bus jockey.

Tales of garage life

We had a driver at the garage whose sideline was selling condoms. He used to buy them by the gross and supply the canteens of Brentwood, Chelmsford, Southend and Wood Green. His motto was opposite to the ice cream man which was "stop me and buy one". His was "buy me and stop one". He carried them in a small brief case where ever he went; he often got out of the cab to utter to the passengers the immortal phrase, "Something for the weekend, sir?". On the late shift in the summer we often went over the depot wall to the municipal swimming pool next door for a bit of skinny dipping. One day the fountains stopped working and they had to drain the pool to find the problem; it turned out the blockage was caused by used condoms. The council took on another lifeguard to keep a check on the public, but we knew it was not them.

We had a bus cleaner by the name of Percy whose whole life was centred round the Army. He used to holler and shout just like a drill sergeant. Obviously we bus crews used to play up to him and every Sunday we had what he called Church Parade – at 6am he would have us marching up and down the depot shouting his orders. One Sunday two police cars came into the depot and when the police got out they were laughing. It would seem many residents in the street next door had wanted to know if World War Three had started! Percy was told to keep his voice down a bit and from that point on, all drill stopped. We had another cleaner Marie, who convinced herself that she was Queen of England and could only be addressed as "Her Mage". She also said she had the title deeds to Buckingham Palace. I said to her, how about if I call you "Du Et Mon Droit"; "what's that, she asked" so I explained it is what appears under the Royal Coat of Arms. "Oh that will do" she said. About 6 months later after she had left the bus company, I read in the Brentwood Gazette that the application by the hotel chain Queens Moat House for a drinks licence had been opposed by Queen Mage. It would seem she went to court as Queen to try to stop the licence. I don't think I stopped laughing for a week! Soon after this she was sectioned under the Mental Health Act; I have a great deal of sympathy for people with mental health problems but have to admit they can make us laugh at times.

The toilet block took up a lot of space at the depot and we were told to reverse buses as close to the wall as possible. But before reversing, you had to look to see if any toilet windows were open and if so, take this into consideration. One day a driver started to reverse and the windows were shut, but at the same time another driver was opening them. When the bus and windows came into contact the whole frame was pushed inside and crashed on to the floor of the urinals. Three drivers came running out in a panic with their trousers round their ankles thinking the whole toilet block was about to be demolished with them inside! On another occasion, I bought a bus in just after the evening peak when the shunter said to me "There is someone shagging in one of them new deckers" *[he was referring to an FLF Lodekka]*. He was aware of this as these buses had air suspension, whereas the old buses had leaf springs, so you could see the bus bouncing up and down on the air bags. He said to me, "If you take that bus round the High Street and back I will buy you a couple of pints". I readily agreed, so he went into the canteen to call everyone out to watch. We got an audience of about 50 and they decided to sing *My boy lollipop* by Millie to "serenade" the illicit lovers; the bus washer also bought his long brush which he washed the top deck windows, to give them a tap. I crept into the cab, got all the switches ready and in gear ready to move off. I flashed the cab light to let the audience know the performance was about to start, then sprung into action. Close doors, start engine, move off and put all the saloon lights on in about two seconds. The singing started while the upstairs windows were being hit. I did not know what was going on but I could hear someone coming down the stairs, so I shut the power off to the passenger doors so that they couldn't open them to get out. Then disaster struck! The traffic lights at Weald Road were just turning to red, so I had to pull up. After a few moments I noticed the red light come on in the cab, showing that the rear emergency door had been opened. Then it went off again, meaning that my lovers had escaped by the rear door and had slammed it shut again. I had to return the bus back to the depot to tell my waiting audience the lovers had escaped. They were all very sad, but the two lovers never came into the canteen again so we never did find out who they were!

Learning London

During the late 1950s I decided it would be a good idea to learn my way around London. To this end I got a job as a taxi driver in Brentwood and every time a job came in for London I volunteered to do it. For weeks I got hopelessly lost and got so angry with myself that every time I came back I studied the A to Z. This went on for about 6 months and I began to despair if I would ever learn, then one day I was driving the taxi down Rosebery Avenue towards Holborn Circus when all the roads I had been down fitted in my mind like a gigantic jigsaw puzzle. I was elated – I had cracked it! From this time on I could go anywhere in London without getting lost. However the City was still a bit of a problem but I worked at it and it was easier to crack than the whole of London.

So when I went on the buses I put it round that I knew London. So one day the Brentwood depot supervisor asked me to do a private hire trip to Gatwick with a decker. This was taking 60 children, 6 teachers and all their suitcases to the airport. When the day came I was given Big Bertha – this was an open platform 70 seater, the only one like it on the fleet [this was 1541, later 2510, 236 LNO, the solitary Bristol LDL in the EN fleet]. Despite being an open platform bus, I was not given a conductor, having to do the job alone.

We piled many suitcases under the stairs while the remainder went up front behind my observation window on the long rear-facing seat. The trip went very well and I got them to Gatwick in good time to catch their flight. In fact it went so well I was asked to do the return journey, a 6am pick up from Gatwick a week later. I wanted to get to the airport and get some food before my return journey so I left the depot at 3am. However as I was driving Big Bertha along the A12 just passing Whalebone Lane, the bell rang twice. To say I was shocked was an under-statement, especially at that time of morning! I put all the saloon lights on and pulled into the bus lay-by at Summerville Road, keeping an eye on the platform at all times. No one got off. No one was sitting downstairs either. So I assumed perhaps there was an old tramp sitting upstairs. I got out of the bus and went upstairs, but there was no one up there either. By now my curly hair had gone straight with fright!

From this time on I drove with all the saloon lights on. All went well until we crossed the river and got to the Elephant & Castle junction. Then a lot of people on their way home after a night on the town got on the bus when I had to stop at traffic lights, so I had to keep pulling over to tell them to get off. Then I thought it would be a good idea to just leave the cleaner lights on [there was a switch which put on only half the lights, enough for the cleaners to work but avoiding draining the batteries on a parked bus].

As I was going through Streatham I noticed a newsagent putting a board out on the street which had on it "Air crash, many dead". My mind went into overdrive and I thought about my passengers, so I decided to get out and buy a paper to check. Thankfully it was not my school group but an air crash in India. At this point I happened to look upstairs, only to see a passenger sitting in one of the seats! I thought "I do not believe this" – I went upstairs and asked where he was going. He tried to give me the fare and said he was going to work. I asked him if he worked at Gatwick Airport – he said no, so I said he'd better get off or that was where he would finish up!

I had "Private" on the destination blind and of course the bus was painted green not red. I did not realise until then that the public could be such idiots. Eventually we got to Gatwick and back and a good time was had by all except me. And I never did find out how or why the bells had rung back on the A12 in the early hours of the morning!

What I didn't like was the way the depot engineers used to cut the fuel pumps back to improve the miles per gallon. The problem was that when you came to a hill, the buses were no good. Now before I worked for EN, I had been a motor mechanic and knew how to open the fuel pumps out with a screwdriver and a spanner. So at every terminus I got busy! It only took a few minutes but the acceleration was much better and we got a higher top speed of 45mph or so.

When the engineers realized what was happening they put a lead seal on the screws on the fuel pumps to stop our unofficial alterations. But I had another plan: by putting an empty cotton reel behind the rack arm, this stopped the vacuum sucker from returning fully and gave us a bit more speed. The downside was that it increased the smoke – on one occasion on a calm day I caused a 12' high black fog behind the bus along Bentley straight mile (the A128 Ongar Road at Pilgrims Hatch)! As I pulled the bus into the lay-by at the Rose & Crown stop, a police car stopped and the policeman came up to my cab window to complain about the smoke. I told him that I drove them, not serviced them, and that he'd better take it up with the garage staff, not with me. Time to remove the offending cotton reel!!

Anyway, he duly complained to the company and back at the garage the fitters took the bus in to be checked and ran it on full throttle (with a brick on the accelerator pedal) for hours, only there was no excess smoke. I managed to convince them that the smoke had come from a tanker on the road in front of me . . .

Read all about it!

What about the time that a newspaper seller nearly caused a strike? A real character called Nobby Clark was a true grafter – by night he worked in Fleet Street "on the print", from 6pm to 2am. Then he piled a load of newspapers into his motorcycle sidecar, to sell from a stall on Brentwood High Street. The stall was kept behind the public toilets and was a double combination wardrobe with the doors removed. One side held the papers, while he could stand in the other half if it was raining. The whole thing was on pram wheels with wheelbarrow handles so that he could move it around.

Nobby used to stand in the middle of the High Street selling papers to motorists stuck in the traffic jams there. When a bus came along he'd be on the platform, selling papers to everyone as they got off. Then he'd go inside to catch those staying on the bus. As a thank you, the driver and conductor would get a free copy of their choice.

On one occasion, returning from a week's holiday, I was astonished to see Nobby with a broom handle with a clip on the end, standing in the road and passing newspapers up to the top deck passengers, who were throwing payment down to him. It turned out that whilst I'd been away, the depot inspector had stopped him going onto the buses, saying that they were private property! I was having none of this, surely the driver is in charge once the bus is out on the road. As the TGWU shop steward, I went to see the boss and we had a hell of a row about it, but he backed down and didn't try to interfere again.

No thanks for the good Samaritan

One day I was driving on the 262 route when I came across a car on fire. The driver was in a state, not knowing what to do, so I asked if the fire was from the petrol or the electrics? (Remember, I'm City & Guilds qualified as a motor mechanic). He didn't know so I lifted the bonnet, to find the battery frying. Using a hacksaw from the toolbox in his car, I was able to cut the positive lead to remove the source of ignition for the fire, then I used the fire extinguisher from my bus to put the fire out.

I duly called for a changeover bus as my bus was no longer carrying the legally required fire extinguisher, and I put in an occurrence form. Two days later I was amazed to get a disciplinary letter, saying I'd misused company property and suspending me without pay for three days! Some thanks for acting the good Samaritan! I went straight to the supervisor's office and gave him a piece of my mind, saying that I'd like to see what people thought when they read about it in the local newspaper.

The winter of '63

I passed my test to drive a double decker for Eastern National on April 3rd, 1962. The winter of '63 was to test my new driving skills to the limit! It froze on Boxing Day 1962 and did not thaw till the following April. It was one of the coldest winters on record in the United Kingdom. At that time there was no salt used to melt the snow, just four men on the back of a Council lorry throwing sand over the road. This was quite useless and eventually the roads became mirrors.

On the day after Boxing Day I was on the 5.10am sign on for Blackmore, the first bus on route 260. However when I went to go out of my front door, I found snow 2ft deep. I did think about not turning out, but this could have cost me a day's pay, as we could only refuse to take a bus out in thick fog and it had to be **thick**. As I lived at Rose Valley, which is within walking distance of the garage, I put my wellies on and turned out. It must have taken me an hour to walk to the garage and by the time I got there I was knackered but assumed I would not be sent out. How wrong I was! Three drivers and conductors had turned up and Inspector Ernie said we had to go out. I told him he was mad but he was adamant we had to turn out. I told him I would only go out if I could take a Leyland Decker, so I took 1136 (FJN 205, one of the Leyland PD2s ordered by City but delivered after the Westcliff take-over) – they were more sure footed on slippery roads than a Bristol.

So with a conductor I duly set off. Now with a whiteout you do not know where the road is and the darkness made it worse. I could only drive at walking speed as I had to keep assessing if I was driving on the road or footpath, and the more we got out into the country, the worse it got. Eventually I got to the Blackmore Road and nothing had been along here, it was a total whiteout. I was worried that I would end up in a ditch – so what I did was to watch the telephone poles and wires – that way I knew that if I kept away from them, I would not be going into the ditch. After about two and a half hours we eventually got into Blackmore (normal running time was just over 20 minutes!).

The publican at the Prince Albert invited us in and gave us a drop of the hard stuff with tea and toast. This was most welcome! We told the passengers waiting there that if they came with us, it was possible they would not get back, as only three crews had turned up. About 12 decided to risk it and got on board. Our return destination was Brentwood Station but I was only going to the Town Centre, as by now I felt as though I had enough, let alone risking going down the hill from the High Street to the station. It took us another four hours to get back to Brentwood as all the idiots had got their cars out and got stuck.

When we got back to the depot we were the only ones who had gone out and got back safely! The conker box (Bristol Lodekka) that went out to Doddinghurst on the 261 was in a ditch and the bus on the 251 was in another ditch near Billericay. After this snow fall the company bought 200 shovels and a lock up shed to keep them in. Conductors had a light weight coke shovel while drivers had a navvy's one. We had to sign when we took the shovels out and again on their return.

DB

1610 – a fast bus

I was reminded of my old pal Lloyd Allen, with one of my all-time favourite REs, dual purpose 1610. Lloyd was such a charismatic man, with that typical Caribbean laid back attitude to life. I never saw him without that broad grin, and nothing ever fazed him, truly a sad loss. As for 1610, I have lost count of the Saturdays that I spent racing up to Hemsby (Gt. Yarmouth) on the old X2 (later 082) on the back road via Bury. St. Edmunds. What a flying machine; on the return journey we would dup an Eastern Counties car. On one occasion the ECOC driver gave up trying to keep up with me, and, during our break at BSE, demanded to know "what the **** was under there?". It was popular on the 2300hrs service 152 to Stock. This ran as far as required, then returned "dead". Usually it only ran as far as Galleywood "Eagle", but one night I had a young couple for Stock, most annoying! As the few remaining passengers alighted at the Eagle, I noticed that they were trying to become intimate on the back seat, with the removal of certain garments. I roared off at full power, negotiating the bends at full speed, and inventing a few extra bends where there was no traffic, in order to make their liaison difficult. After a handbrake stop at Stock, the young lady, on alighting, said "Thanks for the ride", in a most aggressive manner. I replied, "I wasn't aware you got one!".

AT

Driving in a New Town

In 1961 I was living and working in Hackney, East London. The housing situation even then was very difficult. With this in mind I went to Hackney Town Hall where I was given sponsorship forms to work in Basildon. The question I was faced with then was where to work in Basildon. Always having been a 'bus nut' I decided to go to the Eastern National office in Bull Road, Vange, and apply to be a conductor.

After a few days I was invited to be interviewed and fortunately my application was accepted. Between my interview and starting training with Eastern National they had moved into a new depot facility at Cherrydown in Basildon, very close to the town centre and bus station. (The new depot opened at Easter 1961). Despite this matter they forgot to tell me they had moved, as such I arrived at Pitsea Station nice and early. It's a good job I did as I walked down Bull Road, mystified, wondering where I was going wrong, where was that depot? Informed of the move, I then carried on the walk, quite a long walk, from Pitsea to Basildon, on what was quickly becoming a very hot day.

So, how well were we trained? Very well actually, by conductor George Byford, who never understood just why I could do up a 'waybill' so easily. I never told him the conductors at Walton had let me do this when I was a teenage boy. During training there were various forms to fill in, and after a short time if you were satisfactory Eastern National sponsored you for a house with 'Basildon Development Corporation' as a necessary local worker. After seven months I was offered a two bedroom house which I quickly accepted.

The training in the school at Basildon was five days long, there were eight of us in the class and I was amazed how high the standard of applicant was. This was no doubt because of the chance of a house. I was at Basildon depot for a total of six years and as such with so many of the new recruits, having got their home, leaving the company, there was always a staff shortage. This meant, of course, plenty of overtime if you wanted it.

The second week of training involved being on the road with a senior conductor, in my case Harry Millest, a very good man. His driver though,

Harry Risbridger, had very heavy boots which made life very interesting!

The only thing I will say at this point is if you had the 244's, Pitsea – Laindon, via Whitmore Way and Basildon town centre on a Saturday, four or five hours was more than enough. It was a regular occurrence in the 1960's to do over a thousand tickets a shift on Basildon town services. All short fares meant it was quite a game keeping up with bagging your coinage up, however this was compensated with the country routes which were relatively easy.

In 1962, the old system of numbering express services by letters changed to using an X prefix. This meant service D (Southend – London) became the X10. This used the first three coach type FLF's, 1608–10 (184–6 XNO), which later became 2600, 2602 and 2601.

Service D required pre-booking, but when it became the X10, it was opened up to allow passengers to turn up and ride. This made the X10 an immediate success, especially from the Essex end into London.

Basildon initially had three crews working the X10 with Southend having five crews, all on a special rota separate from the main rota. I was a conductor on the X10's, Southend – London service and worked from BN (Basildon) depot. All crews were hand-picked, my driver being Bill Gale, we got on very well as a crew. In charge of express services at Basildon was George Digby, formerly with Digby's of West Bergholt – a very easy-going man and a real busman.

In 1963, Londoners really got to hear of the X10 service and in the summer crews hit many problems on hot sunny days with all the day trippers to Southend. George Digby with Inspector Stan Holder (ex-Walton Depot) listened to drivers' comments and laid on a number of duplicate workings in the Southend direction. The 09:00 Kings Cross to Southend was duplicated from Dalston to Southend and with another duplicate from Leyton to Southend.

However this was still not sufficient. There were many duplicates on other departures. Charlie Gunn at Pier Hill also had the problem at night of getting everyone home, using Southend crews.

After a year, the loadings became so heavy in both directions that three further coach FLF's arrived. 2603 5 (RWC 606–8). Little did I know that I would later go on to purchase 2604 (RWC 607), restoring her to coach condition and rallying her for several years. Out of the three new FLF's, only one came to Basildon, this being 2603, whilst 2604 and 2605 went to SD (Southend) – horror of horrors! However, this meant that 2600 and 2601 transferred from SD to BN at the same time. 2601 was particularly unpopular due to its heavy steering and it being very sluggish. It was the only vehicle which had to use first gear up Bread & Cheese Hill whereas 2603 would go up in third. 2600 was the only one to have chrome wheel embellishments; 2601 and 2602 never did. All later coach FLFs had them.

1964 was a tremendous year for the X10's with much duplication. The 09:00 ex Kings Cross at weekends had a relief (dupe) from Dalston Junction, FLF 70-seater and a second relief from the Bakers Arms at Leyton. It was the same for the 10:00 hrs from Kings Cross. BN also operated the 09:00 ex Southend with two reliefs. The secret of success? A boss that would listen to the men on the road!! And provide the duplicate vehicles, a.m. and p.m. as required. We were on the front line!

This also gave the crews overtime (and the company, huge receipts).

The first X10 rota duties at Basildon were as follows:

Duty 1

07:36 Sign on

07:36 dead: Garage to Basildon Town Centre

07:46 service 151: Town Centre to Southend Victoria Circus 08:46 dead: Victoria Circus to Pier Hill

09:00 X10 Pier Hill to London, Victoria (arr. 11:15)* 11:35 X10 Victoria to Basildon, show Southend (arr. 13:12)

Hand over car Walk to garage

13:17 Spare duty. Work as required 13:56 Sign off

14:06 Finish

* 2 duplicates on this journey at weekends

This was a 6hrs, 40mins duty. When a meal break was taken at the depot, a duty was 7hrs 20mins and not paid, whereas on the duty above, we were away from the depot and paid right through. In other cases, if we worked service 53 for instance and had a meal break at Chelmsford, this would be paid also. This duty was a 'chase', The 151 to Southend would average 150 tickets issued as it was particularly busy from Tarpots.

The 09:00 X10 was full, summer and winter and always a problem with luggage especially at weekends for Victoria. Lots of elderly passengers used the service because conductors were there to help and assist, and because it was a comfortable vehicle.

Other X10 rota duties were:

Duty 2 ~ Monday – Thursday only

13:50 Sign on

14:00 Garage to Basildon Town Centre 14:08 X10 Basildon to Kings Cross

16:00 X10 Kings Cross to Southend (arr. 17:50)* 18:30 X10 Southend to Basildon (show Kings Cross) 19:08 Hand over to Duty 3

Walk to garage 19:13 Spare Duty

20:00 Sign off

20:10 Finish

* 1 duplicate: Kings Cross to Basildon

Duty 3 ~ Monday to Thursday only

16:20 Sign on

16:30 dead: Garage to Coryton, Shell

17:05 service 242: Coryton to Basildon Town Centre 18:05 service 244: duplicate: Basildon Town Centre to Whitmore Way, Grimston Road 18:15 dead: Grimston Road to Garage

18:25 Meal relief

18:55 Walk to Town Centre

19:08 X10 Town Centre to Kings Cross (arr. 20:20)

20:30 Kings Cross to Southend, Pier Hill (arr. 22:20) 22:20 dead: Pier Hill to Victoria Circus

22:50 service 151: Victoria Circus to Basildon 23:50 dead: Basildon Town Centre to Garage 23:52 Sign off

00:02 Finish

Duty 4 ~ Friday, Saturday and Sunday (to cover Friday rest day and to give weekend off) 13:50 Sign on

14:00 dead: Garage to Town Centre 14:08 X10 Basildon to Kings Cross

16:00 X10 Kings Cross to Southend (arr. 17:50) 18:30 X10 Southend to Kings Cross (arr. 20:20)

20:30 X10 Kings Cross to Southend Pier Hill (arr. 22:20) 22:20 dead: Pier Hill to Victoria Circus

22:50 service 151: Victoria Circus to Basildon 23:50 dead: Basildon Town Centre to Garage 23:52 Sign off 00:02 Finish

Basildon conductors had to have two ticket machines. The reason? To take up or finish a duty between Basildon and Southend, we operated a service 151 to save dead mileage. So, a normal Setright Speed machine and waybill was used for this. For normal stage carriage work I had been allocated machine number E1503 from new, which I kept spotless. I was choked later when I had to give it over and get machine number E1010 in exchange! For the X10, Setright insert machines were required. My machine was no. Z27. The other two crews had MB13 and MB14, ex-Moores of Kelvedon machines. Z28 was the spare machine.

These memories give you just an idea as to how the X10 grew from humble beginnings and localised management. Alas, staff shortages came later, and centralised management from Chelmsford took over.

Reflections on the road. I was late turn with driver Roy Hipple (now deceased). Sign on 2.00pm. 2.10 pm car from (Gar) dead to Laindon Hotel, where we handed this car over, for crew to return to BN Garage whom we relieved. We were to take over the 11.30am departure service 53 from Clacton, due at Laindon Hotel at 2.35pm. The crew handed over to us 10 minutes late due to delays in Chelmsford as it was Market Day there. After a few words with the other crew we were on our way with the (LS) leaving Laindon Hotel with a standing load, stopping at every stop on Langdon Hills, where by the time we reached The Crown we were 14 minutes late.

Roy was a flapper and very niggly as a result, it couldn't be helped, due to all the ladies with very much shopping, wound our way through to Orsett where we copped a load from the Hospital for Grays (mainly), always a busy stretch of road this.

Departed Grays 12 minutes late and "flew" to Tilbury Ferry. Arrived 3.32pm, departed 3.34pm (4 mins late) lightly loaded, However at Grays FULL UP, many left behind, including passengers for Butlins at Clacton. This was often a problem on the 53's. Long riders left behind between Grays and Orsett, and so frustrating as on leaving Orsett only a handful of passengers. We kept this motor all the way to Chelmsford arriving on time and handed over to a Colchester crew. We now had time for a well earned cup of tea and a cake. We had a paid meal relief and took over the 5.45pm (service 53) which was the 3.30pm ex Clacton and lo and behold the bus was 25 minutes late arriving at CF. Roy Hipple was fuming! This was due to delays on the A l 2 which were numerous at his time. Anyway this helped us quite a bit as the 6.05 Service 34 was ahead of us to Billericay which cleared most of the road. Roy really chased on and got to Laindon Hotel at 6.50pm (15 mins late) where we handed over to a late turn BN crew also. It was now passenger on Service 244 to BN Garage. walk to Town Centre. Now for some Town work. 7.30pm BN Town Centre to Pitsea Stn, then 7.55pm Pitsea to Basildon (244 Dup this was on Fridays only for some reason) 8.8pm BN Town Centre to Garage. 8.30pm Finish.

With the 53's, five depots had cars allocated namely Clacton, Colchester, Kelvedon, Chelmsford and Basildon. In addition, one Dovercourt car worked the one through journey from Harwich. Clacton depot, always the cleanest vehicles, Colchester the best mechanically, Basildon, well we had the wooden spoon, re-cleanliness and maintenance at this time due to the fact BN seemed to get all the other depots "rubbish".

If you picked up a lot of long riders as was the case at weekends, what a game with all the "fare charts", you can imagine looking up a return from Horndon-on-the-Hill to Wivenhoe! You could always work out how many tickets were issued by looking at the auxiliary waybill, this would be with the vehicle when you took it over.

Reflections on passing points. You may ask what are passing points?

In the good old days of full information for passengers we showed the ultimate destination plus important points on route together with the route number.

Let's start with route 53, Clacton to Tilbury Ferry. Our duty card instructions would be as follows:

From Tilbury Ferry: If only one bus operating would show ultimate destination, normally CLACTON, and passing points:

LAINDON GRAYS

When handing over at Chelmsford the passing points would be changed to:

WITHAM HATFIELD PEVEREL

or on some cars it would read:

WITHAM KELVEDON

On arrival at Colchester for the next stage to Clacton the passing points would be changed to:

WIVENHOE ST. OSYTH

There was an interesting variation to this. If on leaving Tilbury Ferry there was a duplicate vehicle for Chelmsford the through car to Clacton's passing points would read:

CHELMSFORD COLCHESTER

Being such a long route with many short workings there were many variations. For instance, if operating a short from Grays to Billericay the passing points would read:

ORSETT HORNDON ON THE HILL

Passing point blinds were very, very long as there were short workings on most routes to include.

Now let's turn to route 244, Pitsea Station to Laindon Station:

If you had a short from Pitsea to Basildon Town Centre t he passing points would be:

VANGE BARGE WHITMORE WAY

On through journeys from Pitsea to Laindon the passing point s would be:

WHITMORE WAY BASILDON TOW N CENTRE

There was a certain inspector at Basildon Depot who was very hot on seeing the correct ultimate destination displayed and would certainly book you if your passing points were set incorrectly, which is as it should be. For me it was never too much trouble to set the blinds correctly and indeed enjoyed the challenge!

With the many variation of routes it was possible to show something for a passing point and thank goodness very few blinds had SERVICE on them as was Eastern Counties policy, which was a 'lazy, easy' way out.

Reflections on make up points

As a conductor the company required various statistics and information of each journey operated on your duty. I will explain some of what was required:-

Lets first of all deal with route 53, Tilbury Ferry – Chelmsford section.

On leaving Tilbury, in the start column for the start of the journey you would jot down;

1)   Ticket Starting No.

2)   (Pounds) Reading

3)   (Shillings/Pence) Reading

4)   Passenger: No's On Board

START	1	2	3	4	5	6	7	8	9	10
666	692	714	719	741	766	801	808	821		
116	129	140	141	144	152	163	164	167		
16/6	4110	17/4	3/7	18/8	3/9	14/4	19/3	14/2		
14	27	22	12	11	16	37	42	53•		

Make Up Point (1) Grays Memorial

(2)   Orsett Hospital

(3)   Horndon-on-the-Hill

(4)   Laindon Hotel

(5)   Billericay – Sun Hotel

(6)   Stock War Memorial

(7)   Galleywood Eagle

(8)   Wood Street PO

So you can see as the journey proceeded the ticket total was greater from the last make up point and the £ total going up all the time, the pound/pence reading not meaning a lot really.

You will see an asterix by the passenger total of 53 at Wood Street Make Up Point. This signifies a 45 seated full seated load on the LS bus with 8 standing and passengers left behind.

When this happened there was a space on the other side of your waybill for the conductor to report how many passengers were left behind and where!

I am sorry to say that most conductors did not do this part of their duties. I always did, and indeed to prove that my notes and comments were read at Chelmsford Head Office, I was commended by Charlie English, the Chief Schedules Officer at New Writtle Street, for my notes and observations and opinions more than once. He was a very shrewd man and I had the utmost respect for him, no fool, and I have seen him (heard him) really lay down the law to any Depot Union Schedules men who tried to bluff him or pull the wool over his eyes, he knew the Company's routes inside out.

Make up points were all very well on a route such as the 53, plenty of time and distance between Make U p Points, but what about a 'town' route?

Let's go to the 244 from Pitsea to Laindon. The Make Up Points as follows:

1) Pitsea Broadway

2) Vange Barge

3) Long Riding (Staceys Corner)

4) Grimston Road

5) Whitmore Way (Church Road)

6) Basildon Town Centre

Now, supposing you left Pitsea Station with a standing load, no time to Make Up at Pitsea Broadway or The Barge or Staceys Comer, or often anywhere at all on this route at busy times!! So, what did we do?

As soon as you had time you would scribble down some figures in the columns. This was quite easy after a while as, once again, it was a disciplinary offence not to complete a Make Up Point en-route.

TM

Dunmow outstation

Dawn breaks over Dunmow yard,
In comes a cyclist, peddling hard,
Ten to six, that is not too bad,
Oh, what an energetic lad,
Jumps on bus with sprightly tread,. . . .,
Finds batteries well and truly dead,
Oh swear, and cuss, and kick the thing,
Not enough juice to make bells ring,
Back on his bike to find a phone,
And to hear the inspector moan,
Hello Derek, I'm very sorry,
But can you dispatch the breakdown lorry,
And now I dread the coming morn,
When I will face the reg'lars scorn,
'Twas not through me they lost a quarter,
But through a lack of distilled water.

This poem of mine first appeared in Eastern Nationals' in-house magazine "Grapevine" in the late 80s and referred to a true episode when I was providing cover at the Dunmow outstation. Probably it was not a lack of distilled water that caused the problem, but it rhymed and scanned nicely! Hicks of Braintree built a depot at 5 North Street, Dunmow. By the time I joined the company, the garage had been sold to Dons' Coaches, but we still housed a double deck bus there. This operated exclusively on the 33 route between Dunmow, Church End, and Chelmsford. Originally an outstation of Braintree, by the time I was involved, it had been transferred to Chelmsford. The vehicle was a Bristol LD5G, 60 seater, 2508 (1853 F), but was soon replaced by FLF6G, 2848 (MVX 885C). The regular crews were George Latter, and Chris Cracknell, the old boys, and the younger pair Keith Pallet and Richard Wright, known to all as Dunmow Dick. I can still see Chris, a giant of a man, standing on the forecourt at Duke Street, whilst changing the front destination blind, without having to climb onto the step. When the elder pair retired, Dick took up driving duties, and Ray Hitchins, and "Tina" Belsham were drafted in.

I started my PSV driving lessons on my 21st birthday 5/9/1968 and was one of the last conductors to train without pay. At that time the Company had embarked on an aggressive recruitment campaign in the unemployment areas of the North, and a hostel had been established for the incomers to be housed in, pending council accommodation being offered once they had been employed. Naturally the company wanted these through their tests as quickly as possible, for they were being paid. Consequently, I was pushed back for my own test to make way for them. By mid-November, I was getting frustrated at the delay, and made quite a nuisance of myself. I watched as one of the Northerners, Rod Mackenzie, and Dick Wright, went out on Bristol LD5G 2480, for their tests, feeling very angry. I was kicking off alarmingly when they returned, Rod had failed, but Dick was successful, and gained PSV badge FF22859. The examiner heard my raised voice, and offered to take me out, there and then. I had a successful test, being allocated badge FF22864.

Dick passed his test two hours before me but broke his leg later that day, and I had to cover his last conducting shift. I well remember that day! A regular customer was a young lady, Linda Turner, from Great Waltham, who had a penchant for men in busmen's uniforms. She caught the 1305 ex Chelmsford, and excitedly asked if I was to become the regular outstation conductor. I assured her that as long as I was conducting, I would be on the 33 road. At 1525 hrs that afternoon, I operated my first journey as a driver, Sorry Linda! By the time I had to cover a Dunmow shift as a driver, Dons had moved out of North Street to more spacious premises at Parsonage Downs, on the outskirts of town, saving the awkward reverse out of the old depot, under the guidance of the conductor. It was not long until Tina was promoted to Inspector, and Dick went OMO. VR 2027 (NPU 974M) became the regular bus, being suitable for both crew, (Keith and Ray) and OMO.

For a short time, there were two buses allocated to Dons' yard, following Viceroys sudden departure from their Dunmow and Saffron Walden service. Driver Joe Schact was sent in to operate the old Viceroy timetable, using an MW5G dual purpose saloon. At the end of his shift he would take the decker back to the yard, whilst the crews would use the saloon for their evening shift, in order to refuel it at Chelmsford.

Eventually the Viceroy service was tagged on to the 33, and was operated by Chelmsford, leaving the outstation to run the first and last Dunmow-Chelmsford runs, plus the dinner time changeover, and found themselves on Chelmsford town services.

One of my memorable days at Dunmow, was the day after the Christmas holiday. We were operating a Saturday service for the entire week until New Year, so I didn't have to start until 0738. I had abandoned my usual transport, I would normally cycle the 16 miles from my home, but a heavy overnight fall of snow, forced me into my car. 3027 had stood in Dons' yard for three days, and was up to its' axles in snow, but the Gardner engine burst into life. The duty involved the 0756 Church End to Chelmsford, and then the 0845 to Saffron Walden. Progress was steady due to the weather, but I kept reasonably to time. The Radio station, BBC Essex, had announced that the Thaxted to Walden road was closed. The bus route, of course, used the backroads between these points, and a lady in Debden, hearing that the road was closed, abandoned her planned visit to town. She had just taken off her coat, when the bus passed by her house. She phoned the company to complain that I had run, after BBC Essex had said that it was impossible, probably the only time that I was reported for doing the job properly.

AT

Memories – A general assortment

The gang of the 1960s and 1970s. From left to right, the late Bob Beaumont, Brian Barrett, Andy Gipson (editor) and Dave Golland. Seen in front of ENOC Bus No 1541, 236 LNO, Bristol LDL6G at the Walthamstow Pump House Museum on 29th April, 2012. This was the bus referred to by MP on page 55 and by DT on page 131.

A picture gallery of garages and depots

In "The National Way" by Donald MacGregor which marked the Silver Jubilee of ENOC published in 1955, there was a list of existing offices and depots past and present. Many of these have sadly disappeared and only Basildon (new garage opened in 1961) and Hadleigh (ex Benfleet and District Motor Services) remain in 2020. There are some buildings remaining at Bishop's Stortford now a tyre depot; Brentwood, 3 High Street now a retail outlet, Canvey Island, the home of the Canvey Island

Transport Museum; Colchester, derelict and awaiting re-development and at Dovercourt which is now a public library. Buses and Coaches carried their stock number on the front on a cast metal plate. To know where the vehicle was allocated, a coloured background was used above the plate. This was replaced in the 1950's by a black metal plate with a two lettered code and the stock number appeared on the rear of vehicles too. By the early 1960's the stock number and garage plates were red, although some coaches retained cream plates to match their coach livery. Depot and garage codes in the 1960's were as follows:-

BN-Basildon   DT-Dovercourt

BS-Bishop's Stortford   HH-Hadleigh

BE-Braintree   HD-Halstead

BD-Brentwood   MN-Maldon

CY-Canvey Island   PL-Prittlewell

CF-Chelmsford   SD-Southend-on-Sea

CN-Clacton-on-Sea   WG-Wood Green

CR-Colchester

A selection of pictures of those "forgotten" offices and depots can be seen on pages 154 to 158 which includes Bedford depot opened in 1919 and occupied by ENOC from 11th April, 1930 until 1st May 1952 when operations were transferred to the United Counties Omnibus Company Ltd. It is still in continuous use today under the auspices of the Stagecoach East company.

Basildon garage opened on 2nd April, 1961 and is still in operation today with First Bus.

Right: Colchester garage in 1947 looking very clean with three staff in front of ENOC bus No.3476, AVW 454, Dennis Lancet. Situated in Queen Street it was opened in March 1920 by the NOTC. It was closed by First Bus in 2016. The building is now in a derelict state awaiting re-development. A number of archaeology excavations have taken place inside the garage in recent years in view of Colchester's association with the remains of its Roman city which dates from A.D. 43. Part of the south wall of the garage was built on top of the Roman Wall which was built in A.D. 65–80.

An aerial view of Chelmsford Bus Station in 1938. Situated in Duke Street next to the railway station, the pitch roof outlines of the garage can be seen on the left immediately behind the brick facade of the adminstrative offices on the first floor with the public enquiry office and waiting rooms below. The original site dates from 1921 when the NOTC were the operators and it was extensively rebuilt by ENOC in 1936. The bus station and garage closed in October 2004 and then were subsequently demolished before a new bus station with residential and retail outlets was built on the same site in March 2007.

Braintree garage in 1962. This was originally owned by Hicks Brothers who were taken over by the management of ENOC in 1950. The garage was demolished in April 2005.

Not actually a garage, but a turning point with a summer enquiry office at Jaywick Sands near Clacton-on-Sea in 1939. The chalet style building was typical of the 1920's and 30's when Clacton became a popular holiday resort for day trippers and longer stays. The office remained until the 1970's and in recent years the locality is just now called Jaywick, however the sandy beaches remain!
ENOC bus no.3311, EV 5678, T.S.M. B39A awaits departure for the short journey to Holland-on-Sea. No route number is displayed, so the bus could have been on Service 115 via Marine Parade, Clacton or on Service 116 via Clacton Railway Station. No doubt the conductor would have advised intending passengers. Both services would be suspended in October 1939 because of the second World War.

Bedford garage in 1939. Siutuated in St. John Street it is one of the oldest operating garages in England. Opened on 18th August, 1919 by the London General Omnibus Company, the NOTC then took control before it passed to the ENOC Midland Area in 1930. The ENOC Midland Area transferred operations to the United Coiunties Omnibus Co. Ltd, on 1st May, 1952. Today, Stagecoach East, part of Stagecoach Holdings Ltd. continue operations at this remarkable site.

Biggleswade garage in 1949. Situated in Shortwell Street it opened in June 1931. A small garage for the ENOC Midland Area with the vehicle allocation never exceeding 24. It was closed by September 1989 when under the control of Stagecoach East with the site being redeveloped for residential use.

Luton garage in 1938. Situated in Castle Street it was opened in October 1927 by the NOTC before the ENOC Midland Area took control in 1930. It closed in September 2001 after several ownerships since the 1950's. These included United Counties, Luton and District, Sovereign Bus and Coach and Arriva The Shires Ltd. The site is now occupied by a superstore.

Alexander Sagon and a visit to Luton

There was a driver at Colchester, one Alexander Sagon (born 18th March 1893-died July 1963) who never seemed to accept the change to ENOC as he always wore a "National" script style cap badge with similar badges on his greatcoat. During the summer he wore a white inspector's style badge which bore the legend "National 15 Coaches". I knew him slightly but never liked to ask him. Perhaps he was like the Great Western Railway who never seemed to accept that it had been replaced by British Railways (Western Region).

I was demobbed from the RAF in March 1952 and decided to pay a visit to Luton on 30th April, the last day of the ENOC-Midland Section. I had a chat with George Suckling who was the Mechanical Superintendent. He told me he was not very happy with the change and the road staff did not like it at all, as a large number had worked for Road Motors and then subsequently for National from 1924. It had been explained to them that they would still be driving the same buses and the local management would remain, however the United Counties Bus Company were regarded as the "enemy"! I did not visit the area much after that as it never seemed to be the same. No longer would ENOC be seen in such places as Cambridge, Oxford, Northampton, Amersham and Ramsey (not forgetting the Mad Cat Public House at Pidley).

Back in 1948 and 1949, I had a garage pass issued by the late William Morison, Chief Engineer from 1930 until 31st July, 1949 and later renewed by William T. Skinner, Chief Engineer from 1st August, 1949 until 31st December 1962. All in all I was well treated by the Company and travelled all over the system. Alas there is now little left of garage and depot buildings apart from Bedford and the closed Queen Street in Colchester.

JT

My first encounter with Eastern National

In my 'Tailpiece' article in the Omnibus Society Eastern Bulletin number 205 (October 2018), I mentioned our family's imminent move from Bury St Edmunds in West Suffolk to Braintree in rural north Essex. It was circa 1952, when I was about seven or eight years of age.

So it was as I was doing my bit in helping to unload the removal lorry in Church Lane, Bocking that I soon encountered the Tilling green of Eastern National. Despite its name, Church Lane was not some rural backwater, but the B1053 ultimately leading to Saffron Walden, although this was never apparent from any road sign? It was on two frequent routes, the hourly 21 to Great Bardfield via Panfield, Wethersfield and Finchingfield and the mostly half-hourly 23 to Halstead via Gosfield. What a lot of fields, I thought, but this was an aberration – as I believe the only other settlements with that suffix in Essex were the Hanningfields to the south-east of Chelmsford.

This was at a very interesting time, with ENOC only recently having taken over the well-known independent Hicks Bros, with some of its fleet still bearing the erstwhile operator's name. It was either of the aforementioned routes on which I would travel regularly to and from school, although with a lot of folk we would desert the bus for our bikes when the weather allowed.

In the mid to late 1950s my father and I took a couple of short extended tours by ENOC/Westcliff, my mother volunteering to stay at home to look after our large menagerie of pets and poultry. The first was a weekend trip up to Blackpool – northwards overnight on Friday and returning on the Sunday. Unfortunately on this particular Friday night a terrific storm descended upon north Essex, and a second coach (originating probably from Clacton and Colchester) ran into deep floodwater. We were to have met at Halstead and travel northwards in convoy, so we were lucky not to have suffered a similar fate. A later arrival at our hotel (actually in Cleveleys I believe) for breakfast, however, did not dampen our spirits and we were able to have an extremely enjoyable weekend.

Another tour was to North and Mid Wales, stopping overnight at Llangollen, Caernarvon and Church Stretton, and this went without mishap.

On retirement both of my parents enjoyed several Eastern National/Westcliff tours, covering most of Scotland, Wales and the South-West. Personally, I have always admired the neat and functional products of Eastern Coachworks. Nevertheless, I had some sympathy with my parents when they recounted on arrival at some tourist hotspot they felt slightly poor relations when a private operator's luxury coach – possibly Shearings, Wallace Arnold or a smart Southdown Harrington Cavalier – pulled alongside.

PO

The Human Touch!

My conductor, Jim, and I were parked up at Hornbeam Close, the terminus of 262 when a little boy and his Mum got on the bus. He was very talkative and said to me "I want to be a bus driver when I grow up". I said, "do you now, we had better do something about this, come with me", I took him to the cab and made sure the gearstick was not in cog before lifting him in. He sat on my seat and after a lot of vroom, vroom on the steering wheel; I said "don't you think it's time you left?" "Yes" he said. I told him to "press that button" and when the engine fired it startled him a bit as it had now become a vibrating beast.

I asked him to go near the windscreen so I could get in my seat. I told him "from now on you don't touch anything and hold on the grab rails behind, do you understand?" "Yes", he said. At every bus stop he waved to passengers and they were waving to him. I do not know who was enjoying it most. At Brentwood, Mum came to the cab and took him out and when I got out of the cab. Mummy gave me a hug and a kiss. If I had picked up an inspector (jumper) or any office bureaucrats had seen me, I would have been sacked.

I wonder if that little boy became a bus-driver? He probably would not want to do so today with all the rules and regulations!

DB

Cricket, lovely cricket

In the late 1970s EN fielded (pun intended!) a company cricket team, playing a mixture of friendlies and competitive games in the National P.S.V. Knockout Trophy. About a third of the team were from Head Office, another third from Chelmsford depot, and the remainder from other depots. The latter group included Bob Brace and myself from Bishops Stortford. We played all over the south of the country, including at far-away Plymouth and Cardiff. Our transport was almost always RE coach 1610 (GVW 980H).

The trip to Cardiff for the Knockout Trophy semi-final in July 1977 was particularly memorable – we tied (both sides were bowled out for 80) but Cardiff were awarded the tie on a faster scoring-rate. In the evening we were entertained by Cardiff Corporation at their social club, where we foolishly accepted their challenge of a yard-of-ale drinking contest. I have only hazy memories (!) of it, remembering just that they drank us under the table!

On the cricket trips I usually managed to get some bus photography in such as Cardiff Corporation, Guy Arabs at Cardiff Central Bus Station and Eastern Counties buses at Surrey Street Bus Station, Norwich, in April 1978 on the first occasion we played there.

I'll finish by remembering that when LT Chiswick works came to play us at Chelmsford, they came in a Routemaster, which the driver unfortunately tried to take under Duke Street Railway Bridge. After it got jammed there, sniggering ENOC fitters came out and freed the bus by deflating the tyres! I managed to photograph the bus at the match at Marconi's sports ground, with a badly dented roof at the front!

PC

FOREWORD

In issuing the new Rule Book I would like to make certain comments and to offer certain suggestions.

Although, of course, these rules must be regarded as instructions, they are largely intended as a guide for the assistance of staff, and in many cases represent, as I am sure you will agree, sound common sense. Your observance of the rules in the booklet will, in fact, make your daily work easier and, I think, more enjoyable. Some of you will, in the course of the year, come across a situation which is not covered by these rules. The application of your own common sense to the problem, a report or request for confirmation to the nearest official and above all consideration for the safety and comfort of the travelling public, will be a sure guide to your actions. Finally, may I remind you that we are facing a very strong commercial challenge from other forms of transport. The jobs of all of us depend upon the number of members of the public that we can persuade to travel with us, this year and next year, and in the years thereon. If you want to keep, and perhaps improve, the level of employment in this Company, will you remember this, and do everything you can to keep the passengers that we have, and perhaps do something to obtain a few more, and thus consolidate your own job.

R. F. BUSHROD,

General Manager.

From the Eastern National Rule Book For Operating Staff (undated-probably around 1965).

Acknowledgements, Contributors and Picture and Ephemera Credits

The publishers would like to thank the following contributors for pieces written in this book.

RO-Robin Orbell
GD-Geoff Dodson
DW-David Whiteside
BB-Brian Barrett
TC-Revd. Terry Challis
SP-Stephen Purkiss
KS-Keith Shayshutt
MP-Michael Parsons
MH-Michael Harper
DB-Doug Brown
AT-Alan Tebbit B.E.M.
TM-Ted Miles
JT-John Taylor
PO-Peter Offord
PC-Peter Carr

In addition, a special thank you must go to Roger Monk who made available a number of photographs from his father's Alfred Monk "National" collection. Many thanks as well to Roger Barton, John Taylor, Nicolas Collins, Ian Barlex and Dave Golland who have offered invaluable information to ensure publication.

This book would have been impossible without the assistance of Richard Delahoy who as Membership Secretary of the Essex Bus Enthusiasts Group (EBEG) provided an invaluable source of articles previously published in Essex Bus News. Details of the EBEG can be obtained from richard.delahoy@blueyonder.co.uk

Picture and Ephemera Credits

Alfred W. Monk, "National" collection.	**Pages 12, 13 (lower), 17 (lower), 18, 60.**
Alfred W. Monk, photographic collection, courtesy, Roger Monk and the Bus Archive.	**Pages 25, 29, 30, 51, 61, 62, 123, 154, 155, 156, 157, 158.**
Andy Gipson, collection.	**Pages 152, 163.**
Geoff Dodson, collection.	**Pages 10, 23.**
J.F. Parke, collection, courtesy the Bus Archive.	**Page 19 (lower left).**
Keith Valla, courtesy, Nick Agnew.	**Page 63.**
Photochrom Postcard, Alfred W. Monk "National" collection.	**Page 17 (top).**
Richard Delahoy collection, courtesy, Essex Bus Enthusiasts Group and the Bus Archive.	**Pages 13, 16 (upper).**
Richard Delahoy collection.	**Pages 167, 168.**
Roger Barton, collection.	**Page 19 (upper and lower right)**

Every effort has been made to contact all copyright holders. The publishers will be happy to receive notice of any errors or omissions brought to their attention.

Further reading

The following books have been consulted and will be of interest if you wish to know more about ENOC. The Bus Archive which is a sister organisation to the Omnibus Society has within its collections, numerous items relating to ENOC such as photographs, publicity material and publications. You can contact them at hello@busachive.org.uk or phone 01992 629358.

D. MacGregor, *The National Way-Silver Jubilee of the Eastern National Omnibus Co. Ltd. (1955)*

Eastern National Ltd., *Fifty years of Service 1930–1980. (1980)*

Eastern National Ltd., *60 years of Service to Essex. (1990)*

First Essex Buses Ltd., *75 years of Service in Essex. 1930–2005. (2005)*

Crawley, MacGregor, Simpson, *The years between 1909–1969, Vol.2, The Eastern National Story from 1930. (1984)*

D.A. Stebbing, *Eastern National in Focus – Vol.2. (1989)*

R. Delahoy, *Glory Days – Eastern National. (2003)*

C. Stewart, *Buses in Brentwood – A brief history. (2016)*

The PSV Circle, *2PF4 – Fleet history of Eastern National Omnibus Co. Ltd. 1930–1945. (2003)*

D. Moth. *Eastern National. The Final Years* (2018)

The Omnibus Society – Eastern & Southern Branch – *Commemorative Event of the Chelmsford–London (Bow) Route, 21st July 2018. (2018).*

The Omnibus Society – East. Mog. *Bus Garages and Outstations, Trams and Trolleybus Depots of Major operators in Eastern England. (2015).*

D. Thornton, *Just the Ticket (No published date, but possibly 1987)*

P. Wallis, *London Transport Connections 1945–1985. (2003)*

Was this the last ENOC bus in full Eastern National livery with lots of yellow in evidence? No. 3072, KOO 790V, a Bristol VR seen at Bishop's Stortford Interchange in 2010, but where is it going – Stansted Airport?

The last memory for now. First Bus No.37986 Volvo B7TL, Wright Gemini in ENOC Heritage Livery complete with coach fitted seats and showing the red depot and fleet number plates used by ENOC in the 1960's, arriving at Southend Travel Centre on 5th September, 2020. The bus has come from Canvey Island and the driver has already changed the destination blind for the next journey on Service 20 to Hullbridge.